"Superbly written, deeply emotional and empowering, this trilogy is a delightful gift and a powerful testament of wisdom, self-belief, courage, determination and uncommon grace. Joshi's vivid and honest account of her troubled and brave childhood in India, adolescence in London and her remarkable journeys through holy sites and *ashrams* is breathtaking and will keep you engrossed. Her lack of bitterness at the traumatic experiences she encountered as a child and how she overcame her life traumas of self-knowledge and actualisation is truly inspiring and healing, and will surely help others to overcome theirs."

*MonaLisa Chukwuma - Author of 'Define Yourself - and Become the Architect of your Future'*

"Smita has done a wonderful job of telling the universal story of each of our heroic journey home to our true Selves. Across continents and lifetimes, she encourages us to trust our inner voice, so we can heal, find more peace and happiness, and to show up as who we truly are."

*Nick Williams - Author of 'The Work We Were Born to Do'*

"The path to greater self-awareness and understanding that brings us happiness can be rocky and, at times, even treacherous. Smita has been there and got the T-shirt and come back to share the gems of wisdom so that you don't have to do it the hard way. In the *Karma & Diamonds* trilogy, Smita shows how the happiness and fulfilment that we seek are often closer to home than we think. Her account is as entertaining as it is frank. Prepare to ride a roller coaster with her."

*Tom Evans - Author of 'New Magic for a New Era'*

"A page turner with a difference. Smita Joshi has given us an absorbing, heart-warming and inspirational account of how it's indeed possible, with vision and self-belief, to rise above the challenges of life and succeed with gusto.

*Karma & Diamonds* is a gripping trilogy about the struggles of a courageous woman conquering the challenges life throws at her. A whirlwind storyline packed with travel, action and emotion, it is often funny but will drive most of us to tears as we identify with the characters and witness many tragic events Smita gets confronted with. Yet, her journey is inspiring and optimistic."

*Arvind Devalia - Author of the Amazon bestseller 'Get the Life you Love'*

"Without ever preaching, Smita inspires and enlightens the reader to connect to their own inner Self and live life fulfilled. She shows how it's possible to collaborate with the inner Self, even in the most dire of circumstances, to create powerful, wholesome outcomes. Read it as just an engrossing story or allow its deeper messages to alter you forever. One thing is for sure, you will be not escape being touched and blown away by this unique story."

*Chris Day - Author of 'Turning your Knowledge into Income'*

"In this series of books, Smita Joshi has gifted us with an opportunity to follow the struggles of a young British Indian girl as she navigates family tragedy and upheaval, deep traditional expectations and massive inter-cultural differences - whilst at the same time fighting a never-ending battle to trace her own unique path into womanhood, financial success and spiritual freedom.

It is a gem of a tale to inspire all those seeking to transcend limitation, both inner and outer, and all those seeking to become the ultimate source of their own truth and power."

*Robert Thé - Anthropologist*

"I loved the *Karma & Diamonds* Trilogy. This is a heart-warming and true-to-life account of the life and spiritual journey of a brave and determined young British Indian woman.

Book One, *Moon Child*, chronicles Smita's life from a trauma in early childhood to the difficult move from India to England in her early teens, and on into young adulthood, where she realises that to find any peace she has to take a huge leap into the unknown.

Book Two, *Web of Karma*, follows Smita as a young woman on a spiritual journey who also has to develop and grow within a cut-throat and male-dominated business arena. She has to learn how to synchronise her inner spiritual life with the outer mundane one. In this book, Smita faces her demons not only from this life, but from past existences too. At the end of all this, she then finds herself with a life-threatening illness to deal with.

Book Three, *Diamond Revealed*, shows Smita's steady spiritual growth and physical recovery as she becomes more in tune with what she calls her 'Inner Diamond'. Just when she thought her life was predictable, love comes her way. She now has to learn to navigate this new aspect to life, while continuing to integrate the mundane with the spiritual. Old doubts spring up, and Smita has to dive deep in order to feel her way forward.

All throughout these three books, Smita is deeply connected to her own on board *"Guru"*, and is always seeking a deeper meaning to her life and existence. While a serious, and at times heart-wrenching book, it also has a wonderful thread of humour woven through. The author has been courageously honest in her accounting, which leaves the reader with a strong connection not only to the story but to this amazing woman too. The character building and scene setting are excellently written, and draw the reader right into the pages, where they walk over the hot coals right along with the author, and feel her tribulations and joys in a personal way. The examples she gives of her life experiences, and the teaching she receives, are clear and easy to understand, and will provide help and guidance to seekers the world over. Here is an enjoyable and informative journal of how a person can move from a life full of struggles to find fulfilment and happiness."

*Harmony Kent - Author of 'Elemental Earth' and 'The Glade'*

One woman's journey from early trauma as a child in India to discovering the incredible power that lies inside us all.

# Book 1 - MOON CHILD

# Smita Joshi

Published by
Filament Publishing Ltd
16, Croydon Road, Waddon, Croydon,
Surrey, CR0 4PA, United Kingdom
Telephone +44 (0)20 8688 2598
Fax +44 (0)20 7183 7186
info@filamentpublishing.com
www.filamentpublishing.com

ISBN 978-1-910125-62-5

Printed by 4edge Ltd

This book is a work of non-fiction based on the life,
experiences and recollections of the author. In some
cases, names of people,  identifying characteristics and
occupations, places, dates, and sequences or the detail of
events have been changed to protect the privacy of others.
Some characters are composite of several others.

For my Dad

&

With the deepest love and gratitude to
my beloved
Mum,
Grandmother
and
Mahadevi, the Mother Eternal

# Acknowledgements

I have so many people to acknowledge for their love and encouragement in bringing about my project and I am grateful to each one of them.

I offer my heartfelt gratitude to:

Tom Evans, for being an inspirational and exceptional mentor.

Harmony Kent, for excellent editing of the three books.

Pieter Weltevrede, the artist extraordinaire, for allowing me to share his divinely inspired art on my book covers and website (www.karma-and-diamonds.com).

Robert Thé, for his skilful insights with the early version of the book as well as for his practical encouragement throughout.

Arpit Kaushik, whose earliest feedback encouraged me to keep going.

Lucie Feighan, for her priceless insight and friendship over the years.

Arvind Devalia, for being an awesome stand for my completing this book.

Mark Booth, for helping me to shape this book into its current form.

My Love Man, Edwin, whose patient commitment and unwavering devotion pulled me through my darkest moments of writing, when I would rather have given up. I love and adore you - more than I could put into words in any trilogy.

# Table of Contents

# Author's Introduction

This is the book that I wish someone had written for me when I really needed it. The *Karma & Diamonds* trilogy is a compelling and uplifting set of stories about dealing with modern life, stories you want to pick up and be touched and inspired by again and again.

It's a handbook for living the contemporary life while being connected to something deeper within.

The ancient sages of India have described *Atman*, the higher Self, in great detail in the sacred texts. However, accessing it and connecting to it is a whole other matter. Why is it important? How can you access it? How does it look and feel? What difference will it make to be more aware of its presence? What difference will being connected to it make in your life? How can it improve the quality of your everyday life?

I have written this trilogy for those of you who, like me, are seeking to harness your inner radiance and power—whether it be for being more peaceful, feeling more alive and vibrant, or living the best life you possibly dare to.

"You are taken care of—
in the heavens and on earth."

# 1

## *Innocence*

My mum tried to strangle me. I was seven.

That morning, I didn't go to school. Grandma Motima said that I was poorly and had to stay home with her. "You've got a bit of a fever and I don't want you getting worse. Hopefully it's nothing serious and it'll be gone by tomorrow. It's probably because you came home soaked yesterday evening from the beach. What was your Papa thinking, letting you go in the water?"

"Oh, Motima! I wish you had come with us to Chowpatti. It was so much fun," I said, still riding the wave of the thrills from the evening before. "First, Papa took me all around the Maharajah's humungous red palace. He said that no one lives there anymore, but we could still look around outside and in the gardens. We could see an enormous ship going out into the sea. Papa said it was probably taking food and all kinds of things in the Arabian Sea to Dubai from Porbandar Port. Then, just before the huge orange sun went down, we walked along the beach and he let me run into the sea when the waves were coming, and I had to keep jumping up and down to keep my head above them. It was sooooo much fun, Motima! Then Papa bought me some of those delicious hot peanuts with dry, salty skins and even a stick of mango *gulfi* ice cream. It was so yummy."

"Well, no wonder you're sick this morning." She didn't look very happy with these shenanigans.

I wasn't the only one who was sick. A few years ago, my mummy took a turn for the worse. Until then, we'd been constant companions, doing everything together. But then she started to do strange things, she stopped taking care of herself and then, she stopped taking care of me. At first, it was small things like eating in a funny way, playing with her food like a child, and showering less and less frequently. She would get angry occasionally, then more often and, later, seemingly all the time. Eventually, things got so bad that the grown-ups in my family decided that it was best if I came to live with Grandma Motima and Auntie Anna. That was just around the time when I started going to the big school.

When she got ill, Mummy had to go and live at my grandad's, whom we all called *Motabhai*. It means 'big brother' in Gujarati, but everyone in our family called him that. He lived in a lovely big house, just a walk away from our family apartment, where Motima, Auntie Anna and I now lived. We could see Motabhai's house from our upstairs dining room balcony. He said it was better for Mummy to stay at his rather than where we were, because she could be properly looked after over there. Papa didn't live with us either. He went to live at Motabhai's too, because he had to look after my mum. He still came to Motima's for lunch and dinner. That way, he could see me every day, but Mummy wasn't really allowed to visit because she was still very sick. I couldn't wait for Papa to come over to us every night for dinner, because that was when I could tell him, like a non-stop waterfall of words, all about my day at school and what I had done with my friends.

I went with Papa to see Mummy and Motabhai on Sunday afternoons. "Will Mummy be in a good mood today?" I remember asking Papa nervously every time, when he was taking me to see them on the back of his bicycle, but I couldn't wait to see her anyway.

It was a weekly treat to spend time with Grandad Motabhai too. One of my favourite things was to sit next to him on his indoor swing with the padded seat, which hung in his reception lounge. I told him about anything and everything that was on my mind. He listened ever so carefully, now and then saying, "Is that so?" and smiling or laughing at the things I said. I would go on and on until he would say, "Is that so?", and then I would giggle. That was the little game we always played.

Now that I lived with Grandma Motima, I loved my time alone with her. It didn't happen often, because Auntie Anna was usually at home with us too, but today she'd gone to college as it was a weekday. Two of Papa's distant cousins, I called them Auntie Ruhi and Auntie Kala, came to stay with us for a few days once a year. Auntie Ruhi, a married woman who lived near the city of Jabalpur in central India, had already arrived last night, but she too had gone out early to see her friend. Motima had told me that Auntie Kala would be coming today too from Bangalore, but she would only be arriving later in the evening. This meant that I had Motima all to myself, and I intended to make the most of it.

After having a breakfast of lightly spiced potatoes with two yellow *puris*, my favourite breads, that Motima had made for us that morning, I followed her around our bright two-bedroom apartment that was flooded with daylight. Like a baby chick following her mama, I tagged along behind Motima to the bedroom and then into the sitting room, through to the dining room, all the while chirping away, not at all bothered by my fever, trying to engage her in a conversation. With little response from her, I decided to change my tack to please her. I remembered that just a few days ago she had told me, "People love those who work hard and help others." As she went round, first dusting the furniture, and then sweeping the shiny beige floor tiles, I asked, "Can I help you, Motima?"

She squatted with her bum hovering a tiny bit off the floor, doing what to me looked like a funny walk, as she swept with a long, thin, horizontal *saveni* broom. It was funny to watch, because she waddled like a duck while sweeping. To me, the *saveni* broom was like a baby bushy tree, only dried up.

Though still only morning, the summer day was scorching hot, and Motima's light blue cotton *sari* became drenched from perspiration, and tiny beads of moisture rolled down her beautiful soft face. I liked to do grown-up things such as sweep the floor with a *saveni* the way Motima did, and walk around in my auntie's big sandals, and stick on colourful *bindi* dots between my eyebrows just like they did, because it made me feel all grown up and pretty. I could pretend I too was gorgeous like them, or like the Bollywood actresses, Baby Sonia or Zinnat Aman, whose Hindi films we often went to see in the new cinema, close to the seaside by the Maharaja's old palace. Motima didn't answer me when I first asked if I could help, so I asked again, "Motima, can I help you?"

"Here." She handed me a rag, even though she had just dusted. "Go and dust the tables, chairs and cabinets, and anything else you can reach. But don't climb onto the sofa to reach anything, or you'll fall down and hurt yourself." I whizzed around the rooms with the duster and within just a few minutes, I was back to her, twittering away once again.

Being in the house with Motima, I felt warm and so cosy.

I had no idea of what was coming.

"Have you done your *puja* and prayers? I haven't seen you sitting at the altar this morning," she asked, because I actually hadn't done my daily devotional ritual yet. "Why don't you go and do them now? You can do the *puja* for me today, because I'm already late with my chores."

"But I want to stay with *you*, Motima! *Let* me stay with you."

She gave me one of her no-nonsense looks that told me it was best to do as she asked. "And don't forget to chant the '*Aum namah Shivaya*' *mantra* with the *japa mala*. But for goodness sake, don't go putting the *mala* round your neck. It looks like a necklace but it's not for wearing."

"Oh, *Motimaaaaaaa*," I said, exasperated, but in the sweetest way I knew how. "The *mala* is so long. 108 prayer beads! It takes me a very, very long time to do '*Aum namah Shivaya*' with it. Can't I please be by your side instead? I will do it tomorrow when I'm better, I promise."

"If you're well enough to do this incessant chattering," she replied, "then you're well enough to call on Lord Shiva with his *mantra.*"

"Why do I have to do *mantras* anyway? I don't even understand what they are."

"*Mantras* are words with very special sounds. They are the magical keys that open up their very secret powers to you and make you strong and intelligent, like those old *rishis* I told you about who used to live in the forests a long time ago. You can even ask Lord Shiva to take your fever away," Motima said.

"Will I have special powers too if I chant the *mantras?*" I asked.

"Yes, you will. But what's the first *mantra* that you have to do, before you do '*Aum namah Shivaya*'?" she asked.

"Ermmmm ..." I replied, not quite sure if this was a trick question.

"Have you forgotten already? It's the *mantra* for Lord Ganesh. You must always pray to him first and seek his blessings before you pray to any of the other gods and goddesses. And, if you are doing anything special, like sitting an exam, then you must also ask Lord Ganesh's blessings. He will help you to succeed," she said.

"Oh yes, I have to do '*Aum gan Ganpateye namah*' three times." I'd remembered just in time.

"And which *mantra* do you have to chant if you want to be clever at studies and get good grades at school?"

"Oh, oh, I know that one ... that's easy peasy." I replied like a bright spark. "It's '*Aum bhur bhuvah sva, tat savitur varenyam, bhargo devasya dheemahi, dhiyo yo nah prachodayat*'." I felt ever so pleased that I had passed my test in knowing the *mantras* that I had to chant every day to be become strong, bright and smart.

"Yes, good," she said. "And what is it called?"

I thought for a moment, trying hard to remember the name of this *mantra*. "I've forgotten, Motima. Can you tell me again?" I pouted and cupped my head with my little hands, feeling a bit silly.

She gave me a little clue. "It's a name of a *Devi*, a goddess."

"Oh, oh, I know! It's called the *Gayatri Mantra*," I said, as though pulling the answer right out of my hat.

"Good girl," she said, probably trying not to show too much how pleased she was with me. I started towards the corner of the bedroom where our home shrine was placed. "Remember though, that you must say the words with their exact, correct pronunciations, because they are secret keys. If you mispronounce them, they won't have the same effect. Or they might even become harmful."

Our shrine, a wooden case with a pointed dome that made it look like a real temple, was like a doll's house to me. I only had one real doll that my Bapuji, Papa's dad, had sent from Uganda, where he lived with my uncles and aunts. But my only doll was placed high up in the show cabinet, where we kept all our special things that we used only on rare occasions. So, every morning and evening, I played with the golden statue of Lord Ganesh with his huge elephant head and a big barrel belly; Lord Krishna in his cowherd's dress, a yellow tunic and white puffy trousers, playing his wooden flute for his love, Radha; and a silky, bright orange Hanuman Dada, the Monkey God, who held up an entire Himalayan mountain in his hands.

Sometimes, Motima would let me bathe the miniature statues, first with milk and then water, and I would make sure to cleanse Lord Ganesh's little elephant head and trunk with special care. This was because Motima had told me that his dad, Lord Shiva, had chopped off Ganesh's real human head in a fit of anger when he was just a little boy. He and Lord Shiva, who had been away for a few years meditating in the mountaintops of the Himalayas, had not yet met each other.

So Lord Shiva didn't know when he returned home that the little boy who was trying to protect his mother Parvati, and stop Lord Shiva going closer to her, was his own son. Angry at this little boy for blocking his way, Lord Shiva got out his sword and chopped off the little boy's head, only to realise later that this boy was his son.

Goddess Parvati became frantic and inconsolable, and she told Lord Shiva that he *had* to bring Ganesh back to life. He promised Parvati that he would replace Ganesh's head with that of the first creature he saw outside in the jungle, which happened to be an elephant. So, he took the elephant's head and planted it on the boy, Ganesh. Bitterly regretting his actions, Lord Shiva tried to make up for his awful mistake by granting that from then on, Ganesh would have special status in the god world.

For their prayers and offerings to succeed, people would have to ask for Lord Ganesh's blessings at the very beginning of any ceremony or festival before they prayed to any of the other gods and goddesses. He bestowed Lord Ganesh with the power to grant success to any endeavour.

"Poor little Lord Ganesh," I told Motima. "He didn't even do anything wrong, did he? And his Papa still chopped off his poor little head." So whenever it was my turn to bathe the little deities of our home shrine with water and milk, I made sure that I treated Lord Ganesh with extra special tenderness, taking care not to harm his neck and trunk. "Did you miss your Papa when he was away in the mountains, Ganesh *ji*?" I asked him, addressing him respectfully, because Motima had told me that it was rude to call adults, and gods and goddesses, just by their first names. "I know how terrible you must have felt. I really miss my mummy too. Can you *please* make her well again soon?" I poured out my heart to Lord Ganesh. I hadn't lived with my mum since I started at the big school.

Little did I know that, like little Lord Ganesh, I too was about to receive an assault in the neck.

The colourful pictures of gods and goddesses in their small gold and silver frames at our shrine were stories in themselves. The beautiful smiling Goddess Lakshmi, standing on a pink lotus blossom and wearing a rich red and gold *sari*, showered gold coins from her hands. The divine Durga Devi, with her eight arms, carried something different in each one of her hands and wore a bright red-green-yellow *sari*, riding fearlessly alone in the jungle on her powerful tiger. The ethereal Goddess Saraswati, ever so elegant, with four arms, wrapped in a flowing white *sari*, riding her heavenly white swan with huge angel wings that you could almost see through, held a book in one of her hands and played her beloved string instrument, the *veena*, in another. Lord Shiva, with his special third eye, and blue throat garlanded by a black serpent, sat in the Himalayan forest in something called 'snow' on a real tiger skin, just like the one my Motabhai had in the basement shrine at his house.

"Why does Lord Shiva have water coming out of his head?" I asked my Auntie Anna when I was little. She told me that the water was a river called Ganga or Ganges springing out of the snow in the Himalaya Mountains. I asked question after question like, "Does snow only exist in stories or is it for real and where are the Himalaya Mountains?" "Aren't Durga Ma and Lord Shiva afraid of living all alone in the jungle?" "Don't the tigers or lions come and eat them up?"

Sometimes, Motima or Grandad Motabhai read or told me stories about *rishis*. They said these were wise men with a lot of knowledge who lived thousands of years ago in the forests and in the mountains so that they could be alone.

"There, all alone, they could meditate quietly, in peace, where little girls couldn't go to ask so many questions," my Auntie Anna once teased me when she wanted me to be quiet and go to sleep.

When I listened to stories about these *rishis*, I got goose pimples. They were mysterious, magical people, almost like gods and goddesses, with special powers who could bring even dying animals and people back to life with *jadibutis* — potions they made by mixing flowers and plants from the forest. They could see things that normal people could not, like angels and other divine beings.

"Here, Meeta," Motima said. At home, everyone shortened my name to Meeta. "Make these offerings today." She came up to the shrine, handing me a small steel plate with sweets. One was a glistening yellow ball called *laddu*, another a yellow jelly-like square — a small, flat, light brown piece studded with crushed mixed nuts and a juicy, syrupy orange squirly-whirly *jalebi*.

My eyes lit up as I offered these sweets, making the statues of Lord Hanuman and Lord Ganesh, that I was playing with like dolls, fight with each other for the sweets, letting Lord Hanuman snatch away one piece while Lord Ganesh's trunk swiped away a couple more. At the end, there was only one piece left. I shouted from the shrine, "Motima, Motima, Motima! Lord Ganesh and Hanuman Dada came and took nearly all the sweets!" In fact, it was not them at all, it was me, even though I wasn't supposed to eat the sacred offering all by myself. Motima probably didn't hear me, as she didn't answer.

She must be in the bathroom having a shower.

# 2

# *Initiation*

Not wanting Motima to be upset with me, I recited the *Gayatri Mantra* like I was an express steam train racing through the Saurashtra plains. I spoke it as quickly as I possibly could, because I wanted to go and be with Motima again. Hands joined in prayer, I felt relieved that everything she had told me to do was all done now. Then I sprung up from where I was sitting cross-legged on the floor, and made off towards the bathroom. Only a few steps in, I said, "Oh no!" I had forgotten to also chant '*Aum namah Shivaya*' 108 times with the *mantra* beads.

Before going back to the shrine to sit down again to do the Shiva *mantra*, I felt the urge to take a peek through the holes in the stone carvings of our front balcony. It faced out into the alley where our entrance gate was down below. I went to the end corner of the balcony, by our neighbour's door, and looked to see if any of my friends were about. Maybe one of them had also stayed home today and I could ask them to come and play with me later. But I saw only the vegetable man who came round every day with his cart selling fresh vegetables.

As I walked back into the sitting room, someone called from outside, "Smita, eh, Smita!" I perked up, sure that the voice was my mum's.

"Mummy, Mummy, Mummy!" I said, ever so excited, and ran onto the balcony where I climbed up with both my feet onto the small stone ledge so I could properly see below into the alley. "Mummy, Mummy! What are you doing here? You're not supposed to be here!" I asked, surprised but over the moon to see her.

My mum's name, Poonam, was given to her by her father because she was born on the night of the full moon. When I was away from Mummy, I often looked up at the night sky when the moon was full, feeling closer to her, feeling safe for being watched over by my Mother Moon.

"Come down and open the gate," she said. I leapt down from the ledge and went bounding down the stairs as fast as I could. The wooden gate was locked from the inside, so I opened it and ran out to her and put my arms around her *sari*, gripping both her legs. "Mummy, Mummy ... I was missing you so much!"

I hugged her as hard as I could. She didn't look like her usual self. Normally, stunningly pretty, petite and elegant, now she looked thin, her clothes didn't match, and her hair was roughly twisted and tucked into a small bun on the top of her head, but to the side. Unkempt and dishevelled, it was as though she had just left it like that after washing it and then it blew around in a windy storm. Her navy and dark green nylon *sari*, printed with our Porbandar town's famous *bandhani* tie-dye print, was crudely tucked at her skinny waist into a long, grey mismatched petticoat so that one side came below her right ankle and the other side too high, showing the long petticoat underneath.

Even I knew that *saris* were meant to be worn so that they covered your ankles and feet and never showed your petticoat. I knew this because every morning, Motima made me tug at the bottom edges of her *sari* until it was set properly down to her feet. Mummy's short brown *sari* blouse, also mismatched with her *sari*, was missing its last button hook. Unlike other mums, she wore no jewellery except for two large gold hoop earrings. This was not the same stylish mum I remembered from my younger days, who made a big fuss of ensuring that each and every item of her clothing and accessory was impeccably put together.

"I had a dream in the night that you're not well. Are you not well?" she asked in a tender voice, stroking the hair off my forehead.

"Motima says I have a slight fever, but I'm so happy to see you, Mummy." I craned my neck to look up, beaming at her.

"Why haven't you come to see me? Why didn't you answer me when I came here calling for you yesterday?" she said, in a harsh, angry tone.

"I didn't see you yesterday, Mummy. We came to see you only on Sunday, don't you remember?" I felt taken aback and baffled at the change in her voice.

"Don't answer back!" She scolded sharply as she bent over towards my face. "You can't live here anymore. You have to be with me. You're coming to stay with me. I've come to take you away. Let's go..." she said, gripping me by my left wrist, and wrenching and pulling me while she walked towards the entrance of our alley.

My belly felt like it was melting, and everything felt runny inside of me. Mummy's mood scared me and I just wanted to run away. I tried to wriggle out of her strong grip, but she yanked at me even harder, making my wrist burn. "Mummy, Motima will tell me off if I go without asking her! I want to stay here. Mummy, what are you doing?" I was suddenly frightened of what she might do.

"Stop whining and be quiet!" She turned her head, making angry eyes at me that now made me so nervous and frightened that I felt like I might pee in my pants.

"Let me go, Mummy! You're hurting my hand ... ," I said, still struggling to free myself, and crying.

"I'm your mother! Why don't you listen to me? You have to do what I say." She turned around and leant over me.

"Why are you angry, Mummy? Have I been a naughty girl?" I asked, feeling desperate.

No one else was in our alley and Mummy got more and more angry with me, still not letting me go, angrier than I had seen her before, but I still didn't know why. My heart thumped so hard that I felt it might jump out into the street and run away without me. My chest was tight, as if someone had stuffed some apples into it while I was busy being afraid. Mummy's grip tightened around my wrist, pulling me along the alley behind her. I now felt so scared that I couldn't move. I froze.

My body was limp and I was sobbing and sobbing so hard that at times I forgot to breathe. The hot tears that rolled down my face in the scorching summer sun burnt my red cheeks.

"Stop that wailing!" she said as she leant over me, now gripping me by both my shoulders and shaking me, her eyes still big, and on fire.

I was so terrified of what she might do next that I started to scream at the top of my voice, "Motima, Motima, Motima ... "

Angrier than ever, she said, "Stop that screaming. Don't create a scene." But I couldn't help myself sobbing and calling out to Motima.

"Stop it, I said!" She tried to get me to stop screaming, and put her hands around my throat and squeezed, suffocating me—choking me more the harder she squeezed. Frantically, desperately, I gasped for breath. With her hands still around my throat, she shook me hard in desperation to avoid anyone else hearing me making such a commotion.

I struggled, not able to breathe, choking. In between her shaking and squeezing me, in the midst of panic and terror, my mouth desperately gasped for air, my eyes popped out of my face. I felt hot, confused, shocked, dizzy. Everything started to spin around me.

It's all over! This is it. This is the end for me.

Just then, I heard Papa's booming voice as he suddenly appeared from around the corner into our alley. His bicycle came towards us and he was shouting.

"Hey! What the hell are you doing? Stop that! Let her go! Now! Right this second!"

Motima shouted from the balcony upstairs. "What's happening down there? Oh, my God! What are you doing, Poonam? Have you lost your mind?"

Motima came running down the stairs just as Papa was getting off the bicycle, almost throwing it against the wall of our building, and headed straight towards us. He grabbed my arm to pull me away from Mummy. She let go of my throat but gripped at my other arm, and tried to pull me back towards her, but Papa was stronger. He towered over her and didn't allow her to get me. Then he freed my arm from her grip and pulled it away, swivelled me around, put his hands under my armpits, and picked me up, huddling me into his big strong arms, almost pinning me to his broad chest and shoulders.

I was still choking, but with the sudden release of Mummy's hands from around my throat, my mouth tried to take in big gasps of air, making me cough and splutter and cough and splutter. I felt like I might choke all over again because the air wasn't getting into me quickly enough. I struggled for breath for a few more moments, and Papa still held on to me.

He asked her, shocked and incensed, "What do you think you're doing? What the hell possessed you to do something like that?"

"Give her back to me," Mummy shouted, furious at Papa for taking me away from her.

She tried to pry me off him but only managed to get hold of the skirt of my dress, because Papa took a step away from her just in time.

"Give her to me! She's my child and I love her to bits. She's coming home with me. You have no right to keep her away from me. How do you expect me to live without her?" Mummy raged and raged, and it did not look to me like she was going to leave without me.

I couldn't bear this. On top of that, now Mummy and Papa were fighting. I hated this. It was unbearable for me to see them being angry at each other. It made my stomach churn, like there was thunder and lightning going on in my belly.

I wanted to shout, "Stop this, Mummy! Don't be angry with Mummy, Papa!" But the words were stuck in my throat and no sound came out.

Why was this happening? This was all horrible, horrible, horrible. I sobbed uncontrollably, unstoppably, and my mouth opened and closed like a fish, in shock, still gasping to suck in loads of air.

Motima had reached the alley now.

"Take Meeta upstairs. Now." Papa pushed me into Motima's arms. "You're coming with me!" he said, turning to my mum, and gripping her by the arm. "You're coming back with me right now to Motabhai's. What the hell do you think you were doing?"

After that, I couldn't hear them anymore because Motima had already taken me upstairs and sat me on the bed, where I carried on sobbing and trembling. I was terrified and shocked, and just sobbed for a long time as she held me. I must have fallen asleep after that because I don't remember what happened next.

I don't know how long I was asleep but I woke up exhausted, wounded, and hurting as if an elephant had rammed into me. I lay still on my bed, overwhelmed by the fear that churned away in my belly and the deep anxiety crammed in my chest.

What would happen now?

It must have already been close to teatime in the afternoon, as Auntie Anna was back from college. Auntie Ruhi had also come back from visiting her friend. They sat with Motima on the bed across from me, in the only bedroom we had. Motima was telling them about what had happened.

Still lying on the bed, I looked around for Mummy but didn't see her. Auntie Ruhi said, "It's a miracle that Rajubhai (my dad) came home when he did! How come he came home at that time of the morning? He doesn't usually come home until one thirty or two o'clock for lunch, does he?"

Motima replied, "Yes. The angels were definitely at work. I dread to think what would have happened to this little girl if he hadn't come just when he did. I was at the back, in the bathroom, so I didn't hear a thing in the beginning. Raju left some papers here last night, so I should think he must have come to pick them up."

Auntie Ruhi said, "He was a godsend then. How very lucky that was."

Motima sighed. "I don't know why this is happening to us. What sins must we have committed in previous lives for such an awful fate to befall us?"

"Poor Rajubhai," Auntie Ruhi said. "He loves Meeta's mum to pieces. What must he be feeling now? He's such a good man, he goes out of his way to help others. A kind-hearted soul. He really doesn't deserve this."

Motima looked worried out of her mind. "I don't know what to do about this. I wish your father were here. What can we do? What can anyone do? It seems to be all out of our hands. Even the doctors don't know what's wrong with Poonam. How can such a beautiful, highly educated woman, a *lawyer*, no less – how can someone like that suddenly get this way?"

"No one will want to marry me now," Auntie Anna said, sitting on the bed across from mine.

"Don't be so foolish. Of course they will," Motima snapped.

Auntie Anna said, "Poonam Bhabhi was such a stunning, stylish woman and so bright and full of life.

She had such a good sense of humour too. It wasn't too long ago that she wouldn't let Meeta out of her sight. How can this be happening to her? There must be something funny going on. Do you think someone has cast a black spell on her? You know, they're always doing things like that in the villages, *tantric* hocus pocus, putting nasty black magic potions in people's tea and suchlike. Or maybe someone has given her the evil eye because people can easily be jealous of her."

Motima sighed again. "I don't know. Anything could have happened. Anything. Maybe she has some harsh *karma* from her previous lives to live through and resolve. Let's all just pray to God that things work out for the best, for this little girl's sake. Let's hope that little Meeta has good *karma* to carry her through this awful fate."

"Where's Mummy? Where's Papa?" I asked. They hadn't noticed that I was awake.

Motima came over to sit by me on my bed. As loving as she was, she was not in the habit of hugging us. Today, however, she surprised me by taking my little reddish-brown hand into her fairer one and replied, "It's okay. Your Papa has taken your mum back to Motabhai's and he's with her. The doctor must already have been to see your mum by now. How are you feeling?" She put her hand on my forehead. "At least your temperature is back to normal." Motima, usually tough and unshakable, looked at me through the thick glass of her spectacles with a vulnerable softness in her brown almond-shaped eyes.

"Why was Mummy so angry with me, Motima? Did I do something wrong? I *must* have been a bad girl, mustn't I, Motima? Is it my fault that she's ill?"

She pulled me towards her and gave me a long hard hug and said, "No, Meeta. You're a good girl! Your mummy is just not well." I did not believe Motima.

Mummy was not just 'not well'. She was very, very ill and, no matter what anyone said, something must be terribly wrong with her. It made my stomach wrench with pain that after all this time, no one knew what was *actually* causing her illness.

My poor mummy! How must it be for her?

My little heart went out to her and there was nothing more I wanted *in the world* than for her to be well again. Motima said I was a good girl, but how could that be? There had to be something wrong with me for Mummy to be so very angry *with me*. It had to be my fault. *I must have done something really bad*. Maybe that was even why she had decided to go away from me. I had to become extra, extra good. Then Mummy would surely be well again and we could all live together.

"What's wrong with Mummy? Why is she not well? Why did she say to Papa, 'You can't keep her away from me'?" I asked, not really understanding any of this. "When will she be like she used to be before?" I started to cry because, though I was only seven, I knew deep down that things were never again going to be the same as before.

"Don't worry about all that. I'm here, aren't I? I'm your mum now! I will look after you. You have to be a brave girl." Motima said, toughening up again.

*'I'm your mum now.'* The words stuck in my mind like stars stick to the night sky.

Motima urged, "Come on, get up. Go and wash your face and you'll feel all fresh." Before the incident, I had felt so connected with Motima, Mummy and Papa, but it was all different now. Why did I feel so separate from them all? Even if things did go back to how they were before with Mummy, how could I ever trust her after what happened this morning? Could I trust anyone again? If things like this happened in life, what else could happen to me, to Papa, to any of us? It was as if life was a floor that kept moving the whole time, and I had to walk on it without falling.

When I came out of the bathroom after washing my face, Motima and my aunties were sipping from saucers filled to the brim with hot spiced *chai* tea.

Motima said, "I don't know what to do. I feel so worried, but there's nothing I can do! I was going to go this afternoon to the market in town and get the groceries for the festival season. *Navratri* starts next week, and *Diwali* and New Year are within a couple of weeks after that. But it doesn't make sense to go now."

She had finished sipping her tea and sat there staring at a spot on the tablecloth, looking lost. I went and stood by her. Auntie Ruhi suggested, "Motima, why don't you go and do the shopping? There's nothing we can do here right now about what's happened. And anyway, it'll do you good to go out and keep busy. Why don't you take Meeta with you? She could do with a change of scene and you can pop into Motabhai's office. Rajubhai will have telephoned him already so he must know what's happened. Motabhai is bound to be out of court by now and probably back in his office. He must be worried sick too. It'll be good if he can see Meeta."

Auntie Ruhi smiled sweetly at me with her perfect white teeth, then added, "Go on, you two! Anna and I will start making dinner later on."

Motima looked at me as I stood quietly next to her. I felt like someone had put heavy stones at the bottom of my belly and I didn't feel like moving. She said, "Come on, let's go into town then … But Anna, Meeta hasn't eaten a thing since breakfast. Give her some rice and the aubergine and potato curry before we go." Then, turning to me, trying to cheer me up, she said, "It'll make you feel a bit better."

She was just pretending things were back to normal. Didn't she know that things would never be back to where they were?

"Do I have to? Can't we stay home?" I couldn't see the point in doing anything. Despite my pet lip and glum face, Motima was already changing into a peacock-blue organza *sari* to go out. "Come on! It'll do you good to have a change of scenery. Let's pop in to see Motabhai."

We walked to the main road. I wore open sandals and, within minutes, my feet were covered in dust. It was the same main road that I walked to every day with Auntie Anna in the morning to catch my school bus, while she took a different bus to her college.

"Rickshaw *wallah*," Motima yelled out to the autorickshaw driver, calling him over to us as we turned into the main road at the Big Fountain, by the hospital where I was born. The big road went into our town's centre.

"Sudama Chowk," she told the rickshaw *wallah* as she helped me to hop into the cab. "Are all towns as noisy and dusty as Porbandar?" I asked, as I looked at my dust-covered feet, and tried to ignore the intrusive din of the main road.

"Most of them," Motima said. "Porbandar is an ancient town. It's so old that it's even mentioned in one of the very old spiritual books called the Skanda Purana. It used be called Sudama Puri 5000 years ago, because it was the birthplace of Lord Krishna's friend, Sudama."

Then, leaning forward, she said in a raised voice to the rickshaw *wallah*, "Drop us by the fruit and vegetable open market outside the Sudama Temple."

"It will take some time," the rickshaw driver said. "There's a wedding procession making its way through town with a big elephant and horses, and it's slowing everything down!"

"Well then, let's take the road along the seashore and come in through the old part of town, by the main bus station," Motima said.

"We can do that, Ma," the rickshaw *wallah* said politely, "but it won't be much better that way either. The streets are so narrow that side and, with so much traffic, it takes ages to move through the congestion."

We passed the busy bus station where we sometimes went to take a bus to another town or to Motima's village. Then the rickshaw turned into a very narrow street, almost like the alley of our apartment. The enticing smell of hot *samosas* and other freshly fried, spicy savoury snacks filled the small space.

Last time we went past here, I had asked, with my mouth watering, "Motima, can we stop and have some *samosas*?"

She'd replied, "No, definitely not! It's not good to eat such food from outside. They're made by men with dirty hands and cooked in cheap oil. I'll make all your favourite things soon at *Diwali*."

Today, even though I hadn't finished most of the rice and curry Auntie Anna had given to me, I didn't feel like eating *samosas*. My stomach constantly churned and burned, as if little goblins were holding a flaming torch to my wounds. The thought, this is all my fault, drowned out these noisy streets.

We entered another street that looked just like the one we'd left. "Look, that's the Court House, where Motabhai works." Motima pointed to a big old yellow building with a tall wall surrounding it. "Very soon, we'll pass by Motabhai's office."

The rickshaw driver stopped just by the building, which had its doors open, and squeezed the small red balloon near his right hand to sound the horn.

"Come on *Gai Ma*, move!" he shouted to a large cow with long, curvy horns that was having a rest right in the middle of this narrow alley. I could see the bones of her ribs through her brown skin.

"Look there, Motima, aren't those two little baby goats cute?" I pointed to the kids with their mummy goat. They were white and dirty, eating all kinds of rubbish—even newspapers that people had thrown in the street—just by the big cow and by the wall of my grandad's office.

"You clear the way," Motima said to the rickshaw *wallah*. "And we will pop into that office on the corner. Wait for us just there."

We got out of the rickshaw. Now all the motorcycle, car, and rickshaw drivers in this narrow street sounded their horns impatiently. The noise was awful. Even the people on their bicycles tinkled their bells, but the cow carried on happily resting, and the goats feasted on the local scraps. Poor cow. Maybe she's deaf.

I rushed up the steps of Motabhai's office. An old man sat across from his desk, but I ran up to the other side to where Motabhai was sitting. He wore his lawyer's uniform of starched white shirt and sharply creased trousers, also white, with a black Nehru-collared jacket. His tanned, handsome face broke into a warm smile as he saw me and got up from his chair. I almost ran into him, hugging his thin, tall legs.

He picked me up and I burst out crying. I didn't want to but I couldn't help it, and now I couldn't stop. I tried to talk between sobs but the words came out jumbled, "Mummy...Papa...mustn't fight...take home... couldn't breathe ...my fault...get better..."

"Hey, *beta* (sweet child), it's okay. You're safe now," he said, but it didn't reassure me. Motabhai took me through the swinging glass doors into the room. He called it the antechamber. It had floor to ceiling *sheesham* wood shelves full of thick large books that had red, brown and black hard covers with gold writing on them. He sat me down in his big round swivel leather chair, crouched down to look into my face, and smiled at me with so much love and kindness. His eyes were filled with tears too. He gave me another hug. "Everything will be all right. I'm right here for you."

After Motima had done all her shopping at the market, we took another rickshaw to come back home. It was already dark. Every so often, along the way, we heard temple bells pealing and people singing *aarti*, devotional songs, as part of their evening prayers.

At home, Auntie Ruhi and Auntie Anna had made most of the dinner and were rolling out the flatbreads. I liked to pretend I could help in the kitchen. It was Motima who usually gave me a piece or two of the chapatti dough to roll out on a small, flat, round, wooden stand for making flatbreads with a thin, long, rolling pin, but today Auntie Anna held out her hand, offering me two pieces of elastic dough. I shook my head to say that I didn't want to help today, but she said playfully, "Go on, just two and then you can stop."

Auntie Kala had arrived from Bangalore a short while before but no one had yet told her about what had happened earlier.

She walked into the kitchen and said, "Hello! Has someone died? Why the glum faces?"

"Shhhhhh ... don't say that today," Auntie Ruhi said. Before she could say more, Auntie Kala, pinching my cheeks and giving me a kiss, giggled and said, "Look Ruhi, Meeta's chapatti looks like the map of India. So sweet. Hah hah."

Motima replied, scolding her. "Don't make fun of it! That's the way she will learn. She'll be able to make perfect round flatbreads, all the different kinds, by the time she's twelve."

"When I grow up, I want to be a brilliant cook, just like you, Motima." I said, now rolling out another chapatti, and trying hard to be a brave girl, even though I had no idea what being 'brave' meant.

"You've got a long way to go. That one looks like Sri Lanka!" Auntie Anna whispered in my ear, playfully teasing me too, giggling and trying to cheer me up. I was in no mood to be playful or to enjoy their teasing.

"You're horrible, horrible, *horrible*," I screamed, more upset than before, and ran out of the kitchen, straight to the shrine in our bedroom.

One of my aunties had already lit the *ghee* butter lamp and the incense at the shrine, and the room smelt like fresh jasmine flowers. I sat down in front of it, where we came to pray in the evenings, but when I sat down today, I didn't feel like praying.

How could I? The wound inside me hurt as if it was never going to stop. Loud noise filled my head, and thoughts went round and round, like unruly mice. This was all my fault, and I felt more and more angry with myself.

How could I let this happen?

I could hear Motima in the kitchen telling Auntie Kala what had happened. She sounded angry and sad and my aunties sounded upset, maybe with Mummy.

Maybe, like me, they will think it's my fault that she was like that today. Maybe they're upset with me too. I didn't like anyone saying anything horrible about my mum and I wanted to go and tell them to stop talking about her and about what had happened.

The world seemed different from how it was when I woke up. When Motima drew back my curtains that morning, everything had looked colourful and bright. Now everything was grey, lifeless and broken. I felt lonely, even though Motima and my aunties were there, doing their best to look after me. Still, I felt heartbroken. I felt as if Mummy and I were no longer one, like we used to be, and I couldn't bear the thought of it. I no longer wanted Motima and my aunties to see my crying, because Motima said that I had to be brave, and it would give them something else to worry about.

So I took some deep breaths. I would do a long prayer with all my heart for my mummy so she would be better soon. I brought my hands together, closed my eyes and concentrated hard, but no prayer came.

I opened my eyes and stared at the statues in front of me, the ones I had enjoyed playing with every day. They were supposed to be my friends but I felt anger towards them right now. I felt anger towards myself too for being a bad girl.

"Why didn't you tell me that I was being bad?" I said to them crossly, but in a low voice. "Where were you this morning? You weren't there, were you? Because you're not really real, are you? You're just made of clay and marble, just like stone! You're not real! Why should I play with you again? Why should I pray to you anymore? Tell me that!" I stared at the statues and pictures, waiting for an answer, but none came.

"Why didn't you tell me that I was being bad? You didn't care did you?" I continued my tirade against the so-called gods. "How could you let my poor mummy become so ill and take her away from me? And you don't even care that I'm all lonely without her. You don't even care that she's missing me, that she can't be with me, and that it's making her mad. Are you going to send someone who can tell us what's really wrong with Mummy? Are you going to send someone who can make her well again? Are you? Are you? Why don't you? I love my Motima and my aunties and they're here with me, but it's not the same, is it? How can it ever be the same? Is this real life? Is this why you brought me here? Is this how life is going to be from now on? Then I don't want to be here anymore! Take me away! Right now! Or else I'm not going to talk to you anymore! I won't! I won't! I won't!"

While I expressed my desperate emotions and devastated feelings to the deities, I felt as though each and every nerve ending in my belly and chest was on fire, raging in pain. The feelings and emotions I was experiencing felt too intense and overwhelming for a seven-year-old to bear.

Then, I closed my eyes and squeezed them hard, willing the images of the statues and photos in front me to disappear and my sad, irate, upset, unbearable feelings and thoughts to stop. I did this for what felt like an eternity, sitting there with my eyes squeezed tight, trying to shut out the world, being completely on my own, without anything or anyone. The world was awful and I didn't want to be a part of it anymore.

As I stopped squeezing my eyes and let them rest, still closed, an enormous hand appeared in front of me. Behind my closed eyes, I looked at this enormous hand. It held something in its open palm. A little girl! When I looked closer, I was amazed to see that the girl was me! The huge palm moved through the darkness of space and carried me in it.

Then a big yet soft voice resounded in my ear. A voice I'd never heard before. *"You are not alone. You will be well taken care of."*

Startled, I almost jumped up. Who was that? Who did that voice belong to? It was a man's voice, but not Papa's, and anyway he had not yet come for dinner. It wasn't a frightening voice, but gentle and soft, like smooth, comforting, velvet.

I looked left and right and around the room, to see if one of my aunties was playing a trick on me, but I could hear them all in the kitchen. My heart beat fast, but not with terror like earlier in the day. Now, it was because I was excited. The thunder and lightning in my belly had turned to butterflies. A rainbow of colours shot through me and a whoosh of energy filled me.

My spine tingled, as if sparkles of light were making their way up to burst all over my head. The light delighted me and dispelled the fearful, dark poisonous feelings and thoughts of insecurity that had taken hold of my mind and body. I was floating, just like the big hand I had been shown, in this sparkling, colourful cocoon of warm safe love.

The voice held warmth, which soothed and enveloped me like nothing before. The wrenching and aching in my belly and in my chest disappeared and, like ice cubes in the sun, the anger and sadness melted away. My insecurity melted away too. The world felt right again.

I do not know how or why, but I just knew that this voice was true. I closed my eyes again, and brought my hands together in prayer, hoping to hear that soft soothing whisper once more, but I could only hear its faint echo. Even though I didn't know who had spoken, I could trust that voice, I could trust the way it made me feel. It was not going to let me down. I could trust it more than I could trust anything or anyone in the whole world. I was only seven years old, yet I now knew that whatever happened, things would turn out fine.

The gods were not made of clay after all.

# 3

# *Poison*

Papa came home early for dinner, which was unusual. The sun had only just set when I came in after playing outdoors with my friends. Surprised but happy to see him, I went over to Papa and hugged his tall legs, my head reaching some way below his waist.

Grandma Motima had made it a ritual for me to wash my dusty hands and feet after I came in from playing outside, and then to immediately go and sit at our home shrine for my evening prayers. Today, she must have only just lit the *ghee* lamp and the incense as the stick was still burning tall.

As usual, the fragrance of *mogra* (Indian jasmine) filled the air when I came to sit on the floor in front of the shrine. The soft light from the steady, gently undulating, golden flame of the *ghee* lamp gave a familiar *sandhya kaal* (sunset glow) to the room. Our rituals felt comforting and reassuring and, though my mum was still not well enough to live with us, I felt warm and happy, with an unquestionably special feeling that I belonged here.

Wherever Grandma Motima and my Auntie Anna were, I was home.

"Your papers came through today, at Motabhai's office," I overheard Papa say from the dining room, as I was trying to concentrate on my usual prayer to the baby Lord Krishna, for making Mummy well soon and for taking care of Motima, all my aunties, Papa, and Grandad Motabhai. "You can go to London now, as soon as you want to." He sounded relieved. His tone had a smile in it.

Did I hear him say London? I shuffled on my *asan*, the square, woven cotton mat on which I was sitting. "Oh, that is good news!" Auntie Anna said, as she rushed out of the kitchen into the dining room. "Oh, I've been waiting for this for so long! Really, Bhai? Is it really true? You're not playing with us, are you?"

"Don't be so silly! Of course not. I wouldn't joke about something as important as this," he said. "Motima, I think you should go to London as quickly as possible, before there's any change to Britain's existing laws or policies. With all that recent immigration from Uganda into Britain, there's no saying what might change. I'll call Bapuji later this evening and tell him the good news. Then tomorrow, I'll look into how quickly we can get your tickets to fly to London. I should think a month is enough for making all the preparations?"

Motima, seated across from Papa at the dining table, sounded like she was smiling as she said, "I can't believe this is happening. It's been so long in the coming. We haven't seen your father and brothers now for so long that I've stopped counting." There was something different about her voice. She, too, sounded relieved and, unusually for Motima, mellow.

I could not contain myself any longer. Excited, I went tearing out of the shrine room and into the dining room. "London, Papa? Did I hear you say London? Are we going to London, Motima? Auntie Anna, won't it be so much fun to be with all my little cousins? I've seen their pictures. They're so cute!"

"Hang on!" Papa looked stern. "You were not supposed to hear that. You should not listen to other people's conversations. It's bad manners."

"Oh, I wasn't listening, Papa, but I couldn't help overhearing. So, when are we going to London, Papa?" I said, and jumped up and down with excitement.

"*We* are not going. Only Motima and Anna can go." The words came crashing down on me like crumbling bricks in an earthquake. It hadn't occurred to me, not even for a split second, that Motima and Auntie Anna would go somewhere, anywhere, without me.

"No, no, no! They can't. I want to go with them. Motima won't go without me, will you, Motima? You won't leave me here by myself, will you? I won't be able to live without you." I wailed, panic pouring, not able to see how I could possibly survive without them. They were my whole and entire world. I woke up with them and went to bed with them. They dressed me and they fed me. We did everything together. I loved them to pieces. I could not imagine being a day without them, let alone forever.

"You can stay with Auntie Ruhi in Kymore," Papa said, obviously not knowing how to deal with my anguish and torment. "You like her, don't you?"

Motima added, "Remember how she made you that beautiful dress—your favourite dress? She'll look after you and you'll be able to play with your cousins, Payal and Vivek." Nothing Papa or Motima said helped. My panic and fear just grew bigger.

"No, you can't take away my Motima and Auntie Anna," I said, sobbing irrepressibly, unable to breathe, and my face on fire. "I won't stay here without them. You have to send me with them." I ran to Motima for comfort and sobbed and wept into her soft, fresh-smelling cotton *sari*. My world had shattered to smithereens all within the space of a few moments. I couldn't hear what she or anyone said, only that, whatever they said, far from comforting me, they sounded feeble, weak and baffling.

It occurred to me only this way: they were leaving me, and this hurt like someone had cut me in a tender place with a sharp knife.

I was being abandoned. This nine-year-old's fear was being realised.

I was going to be alone and life would never be the same again.

"Don't cry now. Come and have dinner." Motima sounded awkward. "You have your other aunts here and you'll still be able to see your Grandad Motabhai. You'd like that, wouldn't you?"

"Yes, but I want you here as well. It's not the same without you and Auntie Anna." I blubbered, and my nose ran like a river.

"Let's talk about this later. Have a drink of water and eat. You'll feel better when you've had dinner. Look, I've made your favourite *thepla*." She pointed to the pile of lemon-yellow, shallow fried flatbreads. "Do you want some of that delicious *chundo* you like?" Motima reached for the glass jar with the shredded, sweet and sour red mango pickle she had made so expertly herself last summer, as she did every year.

I shook my head. I'd lost my appetite. What use was food to me, now that Motima and Auntie Anna were leaving me behind, dropping me so casually, like an unwanted little kitten? How could they even think about leaving me behind? Did they not see how attached I was to them? Did my affection not mean anything to them? I thought I was special to them. Was that not so? But I know I was special to them. I know, because they had told me so, many times. Had they been lying to me? Did they not mean what they said?

Had not Motima told me that day when Mummy had been angry with me, "I am your mum now"? Had she not said that? Had that not altered my world forever that day, because of what she had said? It had. Because I had believed her with all my heart and started thinking of her as my mum. She was now my mum. Then, how could she possibly leave me behind in Porbandar while she went off with Auntie Anna to London? Why was Auntie Anna allowed to go with her and not me? These questions ran amok in my head, like crazed monkey infants, trapped, unable to get out.

When Mummy had tried to strangle me, Grandma Motima had stepped in as my second mum. She became my 'big mother', just like the meaning of her name, Motima, elder mother. Now, she, too, was leaving me and there would be no one to take her place, and neither could they.

Though I could not have understood it at the time, this turn of events had opened something significant within me, something that would shape my life to come in profound ways and take me on many quests for a deeper, more permanent reality. From the hidden depths of my soul, an old, familiar feeling imprinted in me, and a seemingly indelible *sanskara*, made itself known, once more, whispering to me. Over and over again, it said, "I am not wanted." An old, buried and unconscious, yet fearful sense of not being wanted reared its ugly head.

I was just nine years old, so from where was it coming?

"Come now, come and have your dinner," Auntie Anna said, trying to woo me over to the kitchen, where she crouched on the floor, tending to a pot on the small, clay stove. All I wanted to do was run away, but with Motima, Papa and Auntie Anna all in the house, that certainly wasn't going to happen. "Come. Sit by me," Auntie Anna said kindly.

"Give her two *thepla*, Anjali," Motima said. Anjali was Anna's proper name, but when I was learning to speak, I could only pronounce Anna and not Anjali, and so it stuck as her nickname. "I'll dish up the *chundo* and *rataadu-mattar nu shaak*." Motima spooned some mango pickle and sweet potato and pea curry and took it over to the dinner table, where Papa was seated.

"I don't want any," I said, upset, lingering outside the door of the kitchen, which adjoined the dining room. "My hunger is dead. I won't eat, I won't eat, I'll never eat again!"

"Don't talk to your grandmother like that," Papa said. "Haven't I told you before that we don't talk to elders in that tone and manner. It's rude and disrespectful and I won't have a daughter of mine behave like that." He was right, but I was in no mood at this moment to start removing my shortcomings by learning about the intricacies of Indian etiquette. "Now go and sit at the dining table and have your dinner." Papa, far from being compassionate and being in my world, sounded stressed and stern. This made me want to dig my heels in more. How could he be so harsh? Did he not care that I was hurting?

"Don't scold her now, Raju," my Motima said. "She can eat with me and Anjali a bit later, she's bound to be hungry then. And if she's really not hungry, I'm sure she'll drink some milk. She lives on nothing but gallons of that stuff, anyway."

"I won't," I muttered under my breath so that Papa could not hear, digging my heels in deeper. "I'll never eat or drink again. You'll see."

Instead of going to sit at the dining table, I ran off defiantly into the kitchen where Auntie Anna was still squatting on the floor, watching over a large pot of milk on top of the clay *sagdi* stove. My heart had sunk to depths new to me. Lifeless, starting to sniffle, feeling powerless and frustrated, I threw myself in anger into a squat opposite my aunt, and faced her across the clay stove.

I felt bloody-minded, and a surge of determination welled up within me to teach them all a lesson. How could they even think about leaving me? Just then, a piece of glowering hot coal, about the size of a large marble, tumbled off the stove and onto the floor. Really not expecting it to hurt quite as much, I put my right hand over the flaring red-hot coal. Naturally, it instantly scathed and burnt me, sizzling off a layer or two of my skin. It branded my soft, young palm, and I screamed in agony, sending everyone rushing over in a frenzied panic.

"Oh no! My hand's burning! I'm on fire!"

"What did you do, you silly little thing?" Auntie Anna dashed over to me.

Just then, in the furore as they all rushed to get the coal off my hand, the pot of milk boiled over the top of the solid brass pot and onto the flaming hot coals beneath. It gave off an almighty, unbearable stench like I had never smelled. The blend of vapours from the burnt milk, scalded and seared skin of my palm, and charred coals, gushed into my nostrils. The disgusting odours overpowered me as I desperately took copious intakes of breath of this nasty smell, in an attempt to lessen my agony. Meanwhile, Papa, Motima and Anna scrambled to get me away from the clay stove and boiled-over milk. Papa picked me up like I was a rag doll and rushed me to the kitchen sink, holding my burnt hand firmly under cold running water for what seemed like ages and ages.

My milk years were over. Figuratively and literally. The two things that had been my source of core maternal sustenance, my Grandma Motima and milk, both continued to exist but my relationship to both was altered and would not be the same again.

Far from teaching anyone a lesson, at the age of just nine, it was I who got an early and important lesson of life. I learnt that trying to hurt others because I was hurting was like rubbing salt on my own wounds, or searing my own hand with hot coals. It might, at best, inconvenience the person whose attention I was trying to get, but for sure, it would leave me more injured than before.

Years later, I read an anonymous quote, often misattributed to the Buddha, that resonated this valuable lesson: "Holding onto anger is like drinking poison but expecting the other person to die."

Then I came across another similar teaching, from the Gems of Buddhist Wisdom by the Buddhist Missionary Society, which the above quote was probably paraphrasing. "Hatred is like a poison that you inject into your veins, before injecting it into your enemy. It is throwing cow dung at another: you dirty your hands first, before you dirty others."

"The veils of maya or illusion,
keep us from seeing our true
nature, our essential Self, and
have us seeking for happiness
and fulfillment in things and
people that can never possibly
deliver it to us."

# 4

# Saraswati's Swan

The days leading up to Grandma Motima and Auntie Anna's departure went by as if I was in a bad dream. It would live in my memory like a botched blur that once used to be a near-perfect, colourful painting.

"Be a good girl, now," Motima said awkwardly, as she was leaving. "You'll like being with your Auntie Ruhi in Kymore." Heavy in my heart, I could not let go of my desperate cling to her round, cuddly form. What would I do without Motima and Auntie Anna?

When they went, how I said goodbye to them, details of their preparations, everything, somehow blanked permanently from my mind. The only thing I remembered was that school had come to a close for the summer holidays and, once Motima and Anna left, I was taken by Papa to my Auntie Ruhi's in a town called Kymore, in Madhya Pradesh, in the middle of India. She lived close to big hills, behind which were huge jungles full of tigers. Papa and Grandad Motabhai had hoped that being with my cousins, Vivek—just a couple of years younger than me—and Payal—younger still, would help me to adjust to being without Motima and Auntie Anna.

Though I hadn't spent much time with Auntie Ruhi, I was fond of her and she was kind to me, but still, she was not Grandma Motima. Nor was she my Auntie Anna. The best thing about this move was being with my cousins. I had always wanted a brother and a sister and now, here they were.

Still, I felt heavy, and though I tried my absolute best to be a 'good girl' and be 'happy', so as not to be a burden to Auntie Ruhi, it was hard. I couldn't help feeling sad and lonely. Only at the time, I did not know how to express such complex emotions. It was like carrying around a dense, dark cloud in my heart—a darkness that a nine-year-old could not see beyond, much less dispel. It made me no longer want to play and have fun, like I so easily used to in Porbandar. I remember Motima telling me off, saying, "Stop with that ha-ha and hee-hee now, Tikku, and come and help me with these chapattis," or "Always giggling and being silly, this little one!" Even Motima's stern scolding had felt sweet to me. Nothing she said felt harsh or bitter. She, for me, could do nothing wrong. She was my Motima, my lovely, most wonderful Motima.

Ever since I could remember, Motima had taught me that I had to conduct myself in a way where I was a joy to have around. She had taught me to be helpful and behave in ways where I was not a burden on others. The darkness of the inner world I had been sucked into since Motima went to London, made me feel both guilty and confused. I wanted to be the good girl that Motima had taught me to be, but the darkness had me and I couldn't be my normal self. If ever a little girl needed her mummy, this was it.

Now, everything, but everything, had changed. It would never be the same again.

After the school holidays, I was to go to the same school as Vivek, but then, suddenly, Auntie Ruhi said that her husband, my Uncle Vikram, was going to take me back to Porbandar. "Motabhai misses you and he wants you to go back. He thinks it's best for you to carry on studying at your old school. You'd like that, wouldn't you?"

I nodded. Frankly, I was relieved. Not only did I miss Grandad Motabhai and, though less, Papa, too, I also missed my friends at school and in my neighbourhood. I especially missed my best friend, Deepika. A vibrant and crazy girl, full of fire and fun. She and I, inseparable at school, got up to so much mischief together that, on occasion, teachers ordered us to the naughty corner, giving us the Indian punishment of crossing our arms to hold our earlobes with the opposite hands, then crouch down and stand up a hundred times. Despite getting this severe punishment several times a term, the pay off of doing things we were not supposed to was too tempting that we forgot the shame and pain of our awful punishment. So when, at the start of the new school year, I was back to the English school in Porbandar that I had attended since kindergarten, I was over the moon to see my Deepika again.

Being with Motabhai was like a perpetual *Diwali*, the festival of lights and fireworks, always a special treat and now, for the first time in my life, I was actually living with him. Mummy lived in the upstairs apartment with Papa in Motabhai's big house. The fact that she was upstairs was a relief, because she remained ill and seeing her still terrified me. The memory of her choking me was fresh, as if it had only happened yesterday, even though almost two years had passed. For this reason, she wasn't allowed to come downstairs and I had been told never to venture alone upstairs. This way, when I did see her, it was in the presence of Motabhai and Papa, never on my own.

On the occasions I got to see her, she appeared angry with me and I had no idea why. She seemed to live in a world of her own, a world in which things were different to how they were for the rest of us. Though she seemed to yearn for me constantly, calling out to me, much like a ghost in the house, I dared not go to her for the fear that something awful might happen to me again. I just didn't feel safe around her.

At night, I slept in the second bed in Motabhai's room and, even though the bathroom was just outside his bedroom, I was too scared to go there alone in the dark in the middle of the night. It was as if Mummy's presence was everywhere in the house, even though she hardly ever came downstairs.

School had started after the summer holidays, so I would be away from home from early morning to late evening. Every day, Motabhai would drop me off in his gleaming, new, cream-coloured Ambassador car at the bus stop near the hospital where I was born. From there, the bus took me and other children straight to our school, a few miles outside Porbandar, along the coast of the Arabian Sea. Then, at four o'clock when school finished, I stayed on the bus all the way into the centre of town and went to Motabhai's office, just behind the Porbandar Court House, where he practised law.

"Nileshbhai," he would call out to his clerk, "see what Smita would like for a snack and get her whatever she wants."

I ordered freshly cooked, spicy savoury snacks of one or two small round *kachori*, or *pettis*, or triangular *samosa*, and always one of my favourite, delicious, red apples from Shimla in the Himalayan region. I would sit in the back chamber of Motabhai's office to have my snack, surrounded by floor-to-ceiling shelves lined with his leather-bound law books. I would take a different book out every day and read the legal jargon on the pages, pretending that I was an important lawyer defending my very own client. Sometimes, if there were no clients in his office, Motabhai would pop in and sit with me while I had my snack and quiz me about what I had learnt at school that day. When I finished my homework, I was allowed to come out of the antechamber and sit with him in the main office, where, even though I had no idea what was being talked about, I listened, fascinated to all manner of problems about which people consulted him.

It was a week now, living at Motabhai's. He and I woke up together at seven in the morning. He would have a cup of spiced *chai* and make me a cup of hot milk. In the Indian diet, guided by Ayurvedic principles, milk was considered a superfood. Everyone, including people of Motabhai's age, would have at least one large glass of heated milk a day. Motabhai had his in the evening, after he came back from the office. Sometimes, he would fast by eating just one meal at lunch, made by our cook, Purohit Maharaj, and have a large glass of hot milk for dinner. Motabhai was big on milk and when he realised that I would have absolutely nothing to do with it, he became worried.

"Raju, go and get Smita a large tin of Bournvita cocoa. She likes chocolate and I'm sure she'll be able to drink milk with chocolate in it," he told Papa the first Saturday morning that I had been back.

"But, Motabhai, we've tried everything in the last week. She just won't drink milk anymore." Papa looked at me with exasperation.

"What do you mean, she won't drink milk? Of course she will. She drank nothing but milk all these years. How can a child not drink milk? She must. Get her the Bournvita cocoa and bring it back with you this lunchtime." Motabhai's voice boomed. He had a formidable presence and authority about him and you argued with him at your peril.

I looked at Papa. Papa scowled at me. He was not happy.

Lunchtime came and I had forgotten all about this little exchange between Papa and Motabhai. As I was accustomed to doing at Motima's whenever it was time for Papa to arrive home, I looked out for him and waited. At first sight of his bicycle, I would run down the stairs, shouting, "Papa, Papa! Papa's home," and fling open the gate to let him in. I had developed a similar ritual for him at Motabhai's too. So when lunchtime came, I ran down the steps of the house and into the garden, over to the grilled iron gates shouting and alerting our family cook at the same time, "Papa, Papa! Papa's home for lunch!"

The late summer Gujarati sun blazed directly overhead, making it unbearable to be outdoors for more than a few minutes. Papa entered through the gate I had opened and into the garden. Seeing me approach him for a hug, he glared at me angrily. "Here! You've no excuses not to drink your milk now!" His face dripped beads of moisture from the heat, and his eyes were on fire. He thrust a large tin of Bournvita cocoa powder into my arms, flinging me back. The metal tin dug into my ribs, and hurt me. "Why are you such a spoilt brat? Why can't you be a good girl, like other normal kids, and just drink your milk?" He glared at me, and my legs wobbled like a jack-in-the-box on a wiry coil spring as I tried to move them along to keep up with him, while he rolled his bicycle to rest on one of the side walls.

I felt dizzy and faint.

"Do you have any idea how much this tin costs? It's an exorbitant hundred and five rupees..." He grabbed me by the shoulders and shook me with all his heated frustration. I, meanwhile, looked at him, gripped with shock, dumbstruck. The sun bore a hole in the crown of my head, and Papa's words landed in my ears like burning bricks. Why was he angry with me, like never before? What had I done so wrong? Had I been naughty? Why was he tearing me apart for being a *chaagli*, a spoilt brat, when I was doing my absolute to be the opposite, doing my utmost to be a really good girl?

My legs turned to jelly, while my head rang hollow with the words, "I'm a burden to Papa! I'm a burden... he doesn't want me..." To make my Papa proud with my schoolwork, and recounting to him my little accomplishments, that was my daily occupation, and his anger made me feel ashamed of myself. Not only was he not proud of me, but it was worse, much worse: he was *angry* with me. He was *ashamed* of me.

These unbearable thoughts flashed in my nine-year-old head and, like the sun's rays, bore deep into my psyche in an instant. Stunned, unable to be with the trauma of disappointing Papa, I felt weak and utterly powerless to carry myself and, though overwhelmed by the afternoon midday heat, I froze. The tin of Bournvita chocolate powder escaped from my hands as he squeezed my shoulders with his fury, and my legs gave way. I collapsed onto the hot earth of our garden. The force of the tin crashing to the ground compelled its lid open, scattering the cocoa granules on the earth.

Then, as I fell to the ground, something happened that I will never forget. I felt myself being pulled out of my body, floating in the air, as if there were two of me. One of me on the ground and the other above, outside of my body and up in the air. The higher I went, the cooler the sun became. A gentle breeze blew my hair and I passed through cotton-soft white clouds that made my skin moist, as if someone had wiped my face with a cool, dampened towel. I looked around, only to realise that there was no one else but me. This gave me the strangest feeling, and goosebumps rose on my brown arms.

Should I be excited, or nervous? I looked beneath and saw our whole neighbourhood as a string of joined-up colourful dots. Far from being the large place in which I was used to running around, Motabhai's house had become just a tiny little speck among a sea of dots bordered by the blue blanket of the Arabian Sea. His car was visible, but a bleary fleck, like a full stop, lost on a crowded page. Fascinated, I hung around as time stood motionless.

Then, from behind the light clouds, I saw a small movement. A speck glistened. A glint of sparkling light grew gradually larger as it came towards me, revealing its form. I realised that it was a bird—a large white bird with broad, elegant wings. It looked familiar to me, but I wasn't sure why. Though the appearance of this creature surprised me, it all felt a bit like a dream.

Out of the blinding light of the sun, a magnificent, huge, white swan flew toward me. It clenched a beautiful, large, white lotus blossom in its beak. I recognised it from the pictures on our home shrine. It was the swan on which Saraswati, the Goddess of Knowledge, flew. The bird came closer and looked at me.

*"Hello, little Tikku,"* it spoke to me telepathically. Did he know me? How did he know my pet name?

"Hello!" I said. "You look like the picture of Goddess Saraswati's swan that's in our shrine. Are you the same bird as that one?" Though it was a big swan, I thought it was pretty and not frightening at all.

*"Yes, that's true, that's me."*

"Does that mean I've died and I'm on my way to heaven now?" I asked, hovering up in the clouds.

*"No, silly. Not at all."* It had the sweetest voice. *"You know you shouldn't be up here, don't you? What are you doing up here, little Tikku?"*

"I'm miserable and sad because my Papa is ashamed of me, and I'm a burden to him and nobody wants me!" I was overcome with emotion.

*"Silly! Why do you think he's ashamed of you? He's not ashamed of you. That's just what you think. You are a numpty, aren't you?"* Goddess Saraswati's white swan said, but in a kind, light tone.

"Yes, he is. Why else would he say I'm a spoilt brat, when I try so, so hard to be really good? It must be true," I said, weeping and sniffling, and feeling the raw intensity of rejection. "Motima and Auntie Anna have left me too. It must be because what Papa says is true. And now Papa doesn't want me either. How can I ever be happy now?"

*"Listen to me, sweetheart. I'm going to tell you a secret. And it's a secret that I want you to remember every single day for the rest of your life. Will you do that for me?"* The white swan flexed its huge wings and came closer, shielding

me from the scorching light of the sun with its wings. As it did so, I felt a soothing breeze sweep over me, making me cooler and calmer.

"Yes, I will do that for you." My anguish lessened. More than being afraid, I was suitably impressed by this large, majestic bird.

*"You see, sometimes in life, things are not how they seem. The happiness you're scared of losing is not with Motima or Auntie Anna, or Mummy or Papa. You see, little girl, the secret is that this happiness is already inside you."* Its words were soothing and sweet, like honey.

"But if it's inside me, why haven't I seen it? And why do I feel so lonely all the time? Where is it hiding?" I asked.

*"Ahhh … well, that's something you'll have to look for, like when you play hide and seek and you have to find where your friend is hiding."* The swan smiled.

"Oh, I see." Tears still rolled down my flushed cheeks. I nodded slowly, like I had seen Motabhai do, as if I understood, but fully having no clue. From high on up, I looked down at my grandad's house. Everything looked hazy and distorted, as if I was seeing through a mist. "But why does everything look cloudy and misty? Why can't I see clearly?"

"That, sweet child, is because you're seeing things through the veil," Saraswati's swan said.

"Oh! But, what's a veil?"

*"You know what a veil is. You've seen it. It's when women pull their saris over their heads and then across their face, so that others can't see them and they can only see others like you're seeing now, all hazy and distorted,"* the swan said. *"That's how grown-ups see things in life."*

"Oh, I see." I felt fascinated, even if I didn't really understand. "Is that why it's a secret? Because grown-ups can't see through their veils that happiness is inside them and not outside with other people?"

*"You're a smart little barfi, aren't you?"*

I chuckled. No one had ever called me a delicious Indian sweetmeat made from milk powder. It was one of my favourite sweets. *"So, remember the secret I've told you. And remember, too, as you grow up, don't fall into the trap of seeing things hazy and distorted through the veil. Let the veils fly away, lightly and easily."* The swan fluttered its wings and flew off a little way, before settling gracefully beside me again.

I nodded, taking in everything the bird was telling me.

"Will you promise me something else?" The bird impressed its words on me with such sweetness that I was like a candy-cotton cloud in its wondrous white wings.

I nodded again.

"When you've removed enough of your own veils, will you then help others to do the same and discover their true selves, too?"

I thought about it for a moment. "Will you come back and remind me again if I forget?"

"I will, little one, I surely will. But look what I've brought for you today." The swan came closer still. "Open your hands and make a cup with them."

I did as it asked, and the swan dropped the soft, silky lotus blossom into my hands. "Hold this blossom close to you and drop it inside your heart." The swan said, placing the tip of its beak to the centre of my chest. "It will help you remember what's important in life and what brings real happiness. At times you will forget, but don't worry, when the time is right, you'll remember again."

With these words, it flew up and back into the light, from where it had emerged. It left me with a message that lingered and echoed within me even after I could no longer see its form. *"Remember the words you heard when you were sitting in front of your home shrine, all those years ago: You are taken care of—in the heavens and on earth."*

I then fell back to earth. It was as if my two bodies, the one that had been flying above and the one that had been lying below, reconnected. I wanted to lie there half-asleep for longer, holding onto the fading, sweet dulcet tones of the swan for as long as I could. After a while, I don't know exactly how long, I finally opened my eyes and saw Papa, Motabhai and our cook fussing over me.

When I came back to earth, dizzy and weak, I was lying on my back on the cushioned swing of Motabhai's reception hall, staring at the ceiling. All these worried faces stared at me. I could see their mouths moving but I heard no sound. All I could hear still was the sweet voice of Saraswati's swan. I held onto the melodious voice for as long as I could, not wanting it to go away, but the swan was already gone. Gradually, the sound of that soothing voice receded and, as if someone had turned the volume dial of the radio louder, I began to hear the voices of the people around me. I felt strangely calm and peaceful and wrapped in the soft, beautiful wings of Saraswati's swan, like in a bubble of love, and strong enough to sit up.

I realised years later that, more than its words, this messenger of the beautiful Saraswati had communicated with me by opening something up within my deeper awareness.

I learnt much more about the veils of which Saraswati's swan had taught me—the veils of *maya* or illusion, that keep us from seeing our true nature, our essential Self, and have us seeking for happiness and fulfilment in things and people that can never possibly deliver it to us. In years to come, I would go on travels to understand how these veils became a part of our daily existence, and how they kept us from being fulfilled and, more importantly, how to let them go.

When offered milk diluted with water, Saraswati's swan has the ability to sift the water apart from the milk and drink only the rich beverage, not the water. This swan symbolises that which Goddess Saraswati invites each one of us to develop within ourselves: the ability to discern between real knowledge and that seen through the veil of *maya* or illusion.

"When people are set free to follow
their higher purpose,
they feel at peace."

# 5

## Mother Fire

Shortly after this incident, only days after I had returned to Porbandar and to live with Motabhai, I was told that Papa would be taking Mummy to a hospital somewhere far away in Gujarat. "We will take your mummy to a hospital near Bhuj, you know, a few hours away from Ahmedabad," Papa said, "so that she can be treated for her illness."

"Will she be well again, like she used to be when I was little?" I asked, hopeful, excitement rising.

"I hope so," Papa said, but I could tell he wasn't at all sure after the countless, costly remedies, treatments, doctors and Ayurvedic doctors he and Motabhai had subjected Mummy to. I felt relieved and excited. Even though Papa sounded uncertain, I was convinced that my daily prayers to make Mummy well again were being answered. More than anything in the world, I wanted my mummy back. At last, I would be able to have the hug that I had been longing for and craving in my secret thoughts. Once again, she would be able to be my mum, just like in the old days. We would be able to giggle and laugh and be silly together again. She would dress me up in pretty or fun outfits, and parade me to our neighbours and friends. I had goosebumps just thinking about it.

At the same time, I was relieved for another reason. As much as I missed her and wanted her to be well, what I was really afraid of was being in the same house as her, and with Mummy gone to the hospital, I wouldn't have to be scared. These feelings filled me with guilt. Was I a bad person to want Mummy to go away? Of course, I didn't tell anyone about this. How could I? They would think I was a nasty little girl. And so, it remained my shameful secret.

The day that they were all leaving, Papa came with a car, a driver, and a friend. They were all going to go with Mummy to the hospital. Only when the moment came, Mummy refused to go. She simply would not get in the car. Papa shouted at her. Meanwhile, I looked on from the steps of our house, through the round holes in the decoration of the solid stone wall of our garden compound. I hated seeing Mummy and Papa arguing and shouting at each other and when they did, my legs turned to jelly, making me feel weak and powerless. The neighbours had gathered, and watched as if this was some picture show. It made me wish that the ground would open and gobble me up.

"Motabhai," I said, deeply upset, and tugging at my grandad's spotless white lawyer's trousers. "Please stop them. Tell Mummy and Papa not to shout at each other. I can't bear it." He took me indoors and asked my mum's cousin, Sheetal Masi, to look after me while Mummy and Papa sorted out their differences. Motabhai had asked Sheetal Masi to come and stay with us for a while and to help look after me. She was a sweet aunt and made me all kinds of my favourite foods, even though she wanted to be home in Bombay with her own husband and family.

School resumed that very first week after the summer holidays. A few days after the Bournvita incident and my meeting with Goddess Saraswati's swan, Papa had left with Mummy to take her for her treatment. Just after they left, something horribly unexpected happened.

On the first day of school, Motabhai had dropped me off at the bus stop near the big hospital of Porbandar, not too far from our house, and I got on the bus to school.

As usual, since our kindergarten days, my best friend Deepika got on just a few stops after mine. We hadn't seen each other since before the summer holidays, when I had been taken to Auntie Ruhi's in Kymore. Neither had we written to each other since, and nor was it the norm yet for children to chat to each other on the phone.

On seeing me, she squealed, much too loudly, with surprise and delight, and pushed her way past people standing along the bus. She knocked over, in true exuberant Deepika style, anyone who didn't move out of her way quickly enough. We hugged each other and screamed the roof off the bus with the excitement of seeing each other once more.

"I didn't think I was going to see you again!" she shrieked. "When did you come back? Are you back for good? Will we see each other every day again at school?"

I laughed, nodding. Deepika was such a funny girl, full of bounce and unstoppably joyful. In the tight space permitted by a bus full of school children dressed in indigo-blue uniforms, we jumped up and down and danced our own little dance that we often did in the school playground when we had something to celebrate. Once again, we became inseparable around school, sharing even our packed lunches with each other.

Halfway through the second week of the new school year, and the day after my parents had left, Deepika suddenly stopped coming to school. Every morning, I looked out for her on our regular bus but she didn't get on, not just for a day or two, but a whole two weeks. Neither did I see her older brother, Vinesh, who also went to the same school as us and was a few years ahead. In all the years Deepika and I had known each other, she had barely missed a day of school. Motabhai said that she must have come down with some bug and told me to be patient. At the end of the third week, when I just couldn't be patient any longer, I asked him if he could take me to Deepika's house so that I could see her.

The only thing was, I had been there just a few times before and didn't have her address, but her father had a massive business not too far from Motabhai's office. In Porbandar, even if they may not have met, the senior people of the town knew of each other by reputation. Motabhai sent his clerk, Nileshbhai, off to Deepika's father's business premises to speak to him and arrange for me and Deepika to meet at the weekend.

"Nileshbhai, please can you ask Deepika's papa for their phone number at home, too?" I asked. "Then I can speak to her on the phone tonight."

Excited, I waited at the office for Nileshbhai to return with the good news and ran down the steps of Motabhai's office, but when he came back, he looked serious. "Did you speak to him? What did he say? Did you get Deepika's house phone number? Can I go and see her tomorrow?" I followed him up the steps into the office. "Well? Well, when can I speak to her, Nileshbhai?"

Nileshbhai was quiet. "I think I better speak to *sahib* (sir) first, Smitaben." Even though I was just nine years old, Nileshbhai referred to me courteously as *ben*, literally meaning sister, as this was good manners in Gujarati social etiquette.

"Why? Why?" I asked, impatient. "Tell me now!"

"Smita, *beta*, go and sit in the antechamber for a while," Motabhai said, as he understood that something was wrong. I tried to listen from the other side of the door, but could hear only muffled voices. When he called me to come out, Motabhai sat me down on the chair beside his. The office was already closed to clients as it was now after eight thirty in the evening and time to make our way home. The streets were still busy with rickshaws punching their horns, alerting people to get out of the way, cyclists tinkling their way home and street food sellers pushing their food carts through the street, hoping for their last sales of the day to clear their goods.

"*Beta*," he said, referring to me gently. Something must be gravely wrong, because Motabhai hardly ever called me '*beta*', except in the gravest of situations. "Something has happened. Now, I want you be a strong girl with what I'm about to tell you." My stomach churned and waves did small summersaults. "I'm so sorry to tell you that Deepika will no longer be coming back to school."

"Oh no. Why? What's wrong?" I cried. "Was it something I did?"

"No, no, her papa has sent her to a new school, a boarding school, and it's a long way away, in the Himalayas," he said in a tender voice. Now I knew something had to be terribly wrong, what with Deepika being sent off to a school far, far away and Motabhai being so delicate about the whole thing.

"Why has he done that? Has she been a bad girl? She never mentioned that she was going to change schools. We tell each other everything. And she wouldn't just go, not without telling me." I felt tears of confusion and upset about to erupt. "She wouldn't. She *just wouldn't*."

"Look, *beta*, it's not her fault. Her father made her go suddenly." Motabhai was clearly struggling to explain. "I'll see if you can write to her in a month or two, once she's settled in."

"Why? Why did he make her do that?" Tears poured uncontrollably down my face, as the panicked realisation emerged that, once again, someone important in my life—someone to whom I was close and attached to—had suddenly gone.

"*Beta*, her mother died unexpectedly three weeks ago, and her papa feels it's best that Deepika is looked after in a boarding school."

"Poor, poor Deepika!" My heart melted at the thought of how terrible she must be feeling. Though Deepika's loss was much worse than mine, I had at least some idea of what it was like to be without your mother for long periods of time.

I couldn't believe this turn of events. First Grandma Motima and Auntie Anna, then Mummy and Papa, and now my best friend Deepika, just when I was starting to feel a little better about my circumstances. Life at home without Motima and Auntie Anna was bad enough, but being at school without my best friend as well was unbearable.

In the next days, school lost its lustre for me. There was nothing to look forward to. I had other friends, but they were bland and boring compared to Deepika. She lit up being at school for me. Together we could do anything. I missed her madness. I missed her mischievous sense of humour. She was different to other kids and, somehow, no matter what else was happening, I had the feeling of being warm and happy around her.

A couple of weeks after I learnt about Deepika being sent off to boarding school, I happened to make friends with a girl, a year above mine, who lived in the same street as her. Still missing her, I asked if she knew Deepika. It was then that I heard the real story of what had happened. Chills went down my spine, and I wept for my beautiful friend.

It turned out that Deepika's mother had committed suicide by burning herself alive.

The next time I saw Deepika was when we were eighteen years old. We never talked about what happened to her mother.

"Maya distorts what is real and what is not. It makes you believe that things and people are the source of your happiness and so you become attached to them. It makes you crave and run after what you can't have, and shun what's right and good for you. This makes you miserable."

# 6

## Mother Stranger

With the exception of Grandad Motabhai, every single person with whom I had felt a special affinity had been taken away from me. First, it was Mummy when I was four and, by consequence of her illness, Papa, too. On my fifth birthday, two of my aunts, to whom I was deeply attached, got married and left for their new homes in Mumbai and Junagadh. I was bereft and physically ill for a week after they left. Grandma Motima and Auntie Anna left four years after that, and now Deepika had gone too. Meanwhile, Mummy and Papa had gone off to the big hospital somewhere in Gujarat, leaving me with Motabhai, who worked from morning to night. My time after school, when Motabhai was too busy to have me at his office, was spent with my mum's cousin, aunt Sheetal Masi, and the servants around the house.

It felt like the dark cloud that had gathered when Motima and Auntie Anna left, followed me wherever I went, and with a vengeance. At school, I walked around lifeless, as if the juice of joy had been squeezed out of me. All I felt were a jumble of heavy emotions, too complex for a nine-year-old to comprehend. No one seemed to notice how I had altered from being a vibrant, bubbly child to a withdrawn, sad, little girl. I began to spend more time with my neighbourhood friends after school but, with them too, I had no zest for our daily play.

Almost three months passed when, joyously, Motabhai announced, "Your mum is coming home tomorrow!"

"Oh good. Will she be alright now, Motabhai?" I asked, even though I knew intuitively that she would be fine.

"Yes! I believe she will," he replied, whether he really believed it or not.

My excitement grew over the next twenty-four hours. My mind ran ahead of itself with imagining how wonderful it would be to embrace Mummy again, to be doted on, to be her little girl once more. I imagined her spontaneously cuddling me and giving me hugs when she found something I did funny or smart. I remembered how she used to call me *ustaad pedro*, something like 'cheeky monkey', and how I loved that. All her terms of endearment that I had suppressed by not allowing myself to think about Mummy while she was sick, came rushing back and filled me with a warmth and anticipation. I could not wait for her to return.

"How much longer now, Motabhai? When will Mummy be here?" I asked my grandad as I bounced out of bed on Saturday, waking him up at five o'clock in the morning.

"Still a few hours to go," he replied. "Be just a bit more patient. Go back to sleep for now."

But I couldn't, for imagining all kinds of things that Mummy, Papa and I would now be able to do together. We could go to Chowpatti Beach again on Sunday evenings, like we used to years ago. I could jump the waves again with Papa while Mummy would stand back, shouting, "Smita, oh, Smita! Don't go so far into the water! Raju, don't take her so far into the water!" I smiled to myself, lying in bed as I waited for Motabhai to wake up. Mummy was such a scaredy cat.

I was uncontainable for the rest of the day—a long, long day. Minutes felt like hours, and hours felt like days, as I whiled away the time, waiting for Mummy and Papa to come home. Motabhai didn't know what to do with me either, as I kept jabbering and bombarding him with all kinds of questions about my mum. He had our cook prepare lots of savoury and sweet delicacies in Mummy's honour.

"It's a fresh beginning for all of us," Motabhai said. "Make sure your *samosas* are just so, exactly as she likes them. And remember, her favourite is okra curry, no onions, no tomatoes, just perfectly spiced." Then he went and sat on the indoor swing in the reception hall, next to me, and within moments he was up again, striding out to the kitchen where I could hear him say to the cook, "Hot *puranpuri* today, not just *rotli*." *Puranpuri* was a sweet, stuffed Gujarati flatbread, while *rotli* were Gujarati *chapattis*. Motabhai then came back to sit on the indoor swing, only to get back up again to give some other instruction to make Mummy's homecoming perfect, and making our already irritable cook even more annoyed.

The house smelt more homely than I had ever known it, with the heart-warming aroma of the 'welcome home' feast. All the doors and windows had been thrown open to allow the fresh sea breeze to circulate through the house. Mummy and Papa's apartment upstairs had been cleaned and cleaned again, fit for a fresh start.

Five o'clock in the afternoon finally arrived. Instead of going out to play with my friends, I sat watch at the top of the stairs of our house, having a good view of everything that took place outside on the streets. Finally, I could see the same burgundy Ambassador car that had taken Mummy and Papa away. I got up and rushed indoors. "Motabhai, Motabhai, come! They're here! Mummy's here!" I shouted through the house as I tore around looking for Motabhai, finding him in the basement, bringing out the last of the season's ripened mangoes.

I ran out to the front gate and scrambled with all my might to throw it open. The car had stopped outside the gate and Mummy was just getting out. Suddenly, on having sight of her, my excitement turned, quite out of my control, to a sharp, fearful nervousness. My stomach tensed up. In my mind, I had played and replayed again and again this scene, the scene of being reunited with my beloved mother, where I would run up to her and wrap my arms around her waist and she, in turn, would pick me up and say, *"Taberyu!* Oh, how I've missed you!" *Taberyu*, meaning something like 'cutie pie', was often what Mummy used to call me when she played with me, before she fell sick.

"Ah, there you are, Smita. Come here and give me a hug!" she said, standing at the gate. Her arms were open and she tried to smile, but looked nervous and tense, like she had forgotten how to smile, not at all like the feisty, vibrant Mummy I remembered. Had she forgotten how to be with me, too? Did she remember how she had dragged me through our street, forcing me to go with her? I, too, felt unexpectedly awkward and my body stiffened up as these painful memories resurfaced. A part of me wanted to run into her arms and hug her like never before, like I had imagined and yearned for, but I couldn't move—not my legs, not my arms, not even my lips into a smile. It was as if someone had thrown tight reins around my limbs and bound them motionless.

"Come on! Come and give your mother a hug," this woman said, as she came closer to me. Was that a hint of irritation I heard in her voice? Frozen on the spot, I was fixated on this woman who called herself my mother.

Mummy now looked 'normal' yet there was something very different about her. I recognised her, for sure, but her face had changed. She looked different, and not just because she had put on some weight at the hospital. Something about her composure seemed familiar yet new to me—her gait, the way she moved her head, the way her tongue sat in her mouth, the expression in her eyes; it had all changed. This was neither the mother who had tried to strangle me, nor the one I'd known in the good old days, the one who was so much fun and made me giggle and laugh.

This was someone else, a whole other person, who at one level I recognised and knew well, and yet did not resonate the least bit.

Now that she stood in front of me, my mind was gripped by another, unexpected dilemma. Grandma Motima. But hadn't she told me she was my mum now?

Had I not fully accepted her as my mum? She was my mother. I had to stay loyal to her. How could I have two mothers? Was it alright to have two? Wouldn't Grandma Motima be disappointed with me, after all that she'd done for me, if now I simply forgot about her? That didn't seem right ... My head was a jumble of confusion. I didn't know what to think, and I was much too young to be able to discern what was right and what was not in these emotional matters of such complex humanity.

"Why isn't she coming to me, Motabhai?" this woman said to my grandad. Her question was woven with panic and disappointment, but I sensed her anger beneath the surface, making me recoil even further. I could tell she was gutted. But I couldn't bring myself to go to her. It was too soon.

"Oh, she's just nervous. She's been waiting for you since I told her you were coming, counting the minutes," Motabhai said, gushing with delight to see my mother's altered condition. "Smita hasn't even eaten anything. She said she'll only eat with you when you'll have your meal. Come on, let's go inside."

Mummy and I did not move.

I kept looking at her, almost staring. She no longer looked scary, as I had become accustomed to her looking over the last few years and yet, I still felt afraid of her. If anything, she looked more normal than she had done in years. So why was I not able to go and embrace her? I felt helpless and powerless. A thought, from somewhere in the shadows of my mind, came to the forefront and planted itself immovably. Could I trust her? Would she be able to look after me, this time? Would she leave me, again?

Faint flashbacks of me and Mummy together, crying and screaming, surrounded by a large, noisy crowd in a time and a place that I didn't recognise, gatecrashed in my mind's eye. Was I daydreaming? What on earth were these images? Where were they coming from? Why did I suddenly feel a burning sensation in my throat, as if there was a noose around it?

I couldn't act for my confusion.

She came closer still. I stood motionless, frozen at the garden gates, terrified, torn and confused. Amidst the sheer longing of wanting my mummy back, I had never imagined that I may not be able to bond with her again. It had never crossed my mind that I may resist her, or not accept her again as my mother, or that I may even outright reject her.

She came and placed her arms around my stony coldness. I couldn't respond. And yet, in my heart, I was desperate to hug her and hold her and tell her just how unbearable it had been not being with her all these years. I wanted to tell her about how I loved my time with Grandma Motima and Auntie Anna, and about how Deepika had been my best ever friend, and about the tragedy of her mum. I wanted to tell her how good my grades had been at school and how I always got the top marks in English and maths and science. But I just stared at her like a little rabbit, fixated in the bright car lights on a dark road, unable to know which way to run.

"What's the matter with you? Aren't you happy to see me? I'm your mummy, remember?" Her disappointment made her tongue a little sharp.

"No, no." Motabhai tried to restore balance. "She's barely been able to sleep or do anything since she found out you were coming."

"Then why is she behaving like this? *Tofani!*" The rebuke in her voice was clear. "Is this how it's going to be from now on?"

Who was this woman, calling herself my mummy? *Tofani* means a badly behaved or naughty child. How could she say that? It felt like a grave accusation and a horribly unfair one. How hard I had tried not to be just that. This woman didn't know me at all! Hurt by her sharpness and lack of understanding, I ran away from her, and fled all the way up the stairs that I had not been allowed to go up for so many years, to the rooftop terrace, where I pinned myself in a corner.

I was thrown deep into befuddlement. I had expected my mother to be restored to her former glory, to look the same as before she fell sick, to feel the same to me as when I played with her all those years ago, to behave the same. But she had changed. It all seemed different somehow. In the five years I had been separated from her, I, too, must have appeared changed beyond recognition. We had expected to pick up where we had left off, but life had thrown us all off course and erected between us a chasm that neither could have expected.

It took a few minutes before they all found their way up to me. Seeing Mummy again, I wanted to be happy, hug her, run around her with joy, and cry to let rip years of sadness and loneliness, all at once. Far from being bad, I was terribly mixed up. Confused with all that had gone on in my young life. Confused with the feelings that I did not understand. Confused about things that I would not understand until much, much later in my life.

Overwhelmed and dazed with the sheer multitude of feelings that were erupting within me, I sat in the corner of the open terrace. Instead of finding their natural outlet, these feelings and avalanche of emotions became stifled and stuck within me. In those moments between seeing Mummy emerging from the car and the moment she, Motabhai and Papa reached the rooftop terrace to find me skulking in the corner, the shape of my inner world had been further cast.

So had my relationship with my mother. It would take many years into my adulthood, many solitary years of soul searching and healing, before I would find my way to resolving the trauma that had built up within my foundational first nine years on the planet. Later, I would come to realise that as a child, I could not cope with the deep changes that my mum had undergone. I did not realise then that although she looked different and seemed to behave differently at first sight, deep down she was my same old mummy.

Instead of a happy reunion, a new and unexpected phase of *kismet* or fate had begun. It would be one of unravelling the weave of ancient *karma* that, unbeknownst to us, bound me and my mother through shared experiences in a time beyond the now. In the years to come, its healing was to take me on a journey that would teach me about the web of *karma*, how it binds us, and discovering the source of real happiness and freedom.

"The real question your
soul longs for you to answer
in this lifetime is:
How can I experience the
essence of Who I Am?"

# 7

## *London Calling*

Whatever they did at that Gujarati hospital to my mother, the treatment had worked wonders. She became calmer, more in possession of herself and more 'normal'. She no longer needed to be kept apart from the me and she started to settle into the everyday routine of life. She dressed beautifully again, applying her talent for refined aesthetics. Of course, she still had to take her prescribed medicines, but whatever she was taking, it allowed her mind to be settled and able to function normally in the real world.

Slowly, she started to meet family and community members, too. That disturbed me at times because I could see that people often came to visit her, not out of genuine affection or concern, but out of mere curiosity. I wanted to shout at those people and tell them to go away, that my mother was not some specimen for their nosey, empty entertainment. I would initially feel anger towards them and instinctively want to go and give them a good beating with my fists to make them respect my mum.

No matter how hard I tried, I was not able to bond with her yet, as I had dreamt I would. I wanted to be sweet and kind to her but instead, I found myself answering back and rebelling and provoking her. If she wanted me to do something, I would deliberately not do it. If she called out to me, I would not answer. If she wanted me to go somewhere with her, I would dig my heels in and not go. In fact, my entire relationship with her became one of resisting, answering back, and generally being annoying or annoyed with her. The worst part about this was that I had no idea what had made me behave like this. It made me feel terrible about myself. I felt frustrated because this was not my natural way. A large part of me still couldn't trust her to look after me, but the better behaved I tried to be with her, the less I was able to be. It was as if something within, that I didn't understand, much less control, had hold of me.

No one else seemed to notice or be able to help, either.

"Look, Motabhai," Mummy would complain. "Look how badly behaved she is."

Mummy complained about me to whoever would listen. "Look, Raju, she's being rude to me again." Or, "Look, Sheetal, she's running off without asking me again." The more Mummy complained about me, the more I behaved badly. It was as if I was now recoiling and rebounding from the absolute necessity of having to be the 'good' girl, driven by a subconscious fear of being 'thrown out' if I was too much trouble.

My mother's complaints stirred up and aggravated deep, buried, primal emotions in me but I did not understand, then, why and where they came from. Why was I so angry with her? Later, in my twenties, as I started to look inward for the answers, I realised that all I needed was for her to come back into my world, that of a bright, intelligent but wounded nine-year-old, and re-establish her trust slowly, patiently, with compassion. Mummy's health might have been better, but my scars and confusion were still there from the traumas of the last five years. And, as I would later discover, much beyond.

The child in me needed to be able to behave as badly as I knew how and know that I was still loved and *accepted* just as when I was the 'good' girl. Subconsciously, there was an inborn craving to know that this woman who claimed to be my mother was trustworthy of taking care of and protecting me, no matter what.

If only I or my mum or *someone* had understood then, that what all the badness and complaining was crying out for was nothing more than my pain of separation, and my mother's profound guilt for the way she had behaved towards me. Later, I was to find even deeper reasons for the dynamics that were driving this fledgling mother-daughter relationship. In the absence, however, of such emotional intelligence and higher wisdom, I became a perpetual complaint for Mummy, and she, an annoyance and irritation to me.

The reality was, as much as we would have liked otherwise, nothing in our lives was the same as it had been five years ago. Those years were lost to us forever and we both needed time to accept the tragedy of what had happened, heal that past, and learn to adjust to our new circumstances.

A few months later, almost to the day one year after Motima and Auntie Anna had left for London, Papa came home and announced, "We've got our final papers! We're going to go to live in London!" I had no idea that he was even thinking about taking us to London, but I needed no explanation. "Really? Are you absolutely sure, Papa? Are we really going to live in London? Will we live with Motima and Auntie Anna again? Can we? Can we?" I asked, high as a kite.

Three months on, in late July of 1975, in high, sunny summer of Great Britain, we were on a flight, via Bahrain, to London. This was a huge step for my parents and for me. The rest of our family had already gathered there from Africa, having fled from Idi Amin's purge of Ugandan Asians in 1972. Papa's father, Bapuji, and his brothers had already become settled in London over the last three years. One of Papa's younger brothers, Uncle Sai, had come to London even a few years before 1972 to study and work. It was in his house that we all came together, all fourteen of us. My parents, me, grandparents, four uncles, three aunts and three cousins. My parents, uncles and aunts also had rented rooms nearby but they all came together for dinner every day. I thought I had died and gone to heaven, cocooned in this crowded, busy and cosiest of homes. I shared a tiny little box room with my Auntie Anna, her on the lower bunk bed and me high on up. Being back with Grandma Motima was a dream that I never expected to happen. I was so delighted to see her and my Auntie Anna that nothing, but nothing else mattered.

It also gave me the opportunity to hide in the crowd, away from Papa and Mummy, with whom I still felt distant. Having Grandma Motima back, I felt justified in keeping my distance from Mummy.

London was a wonderful, exciting and fascinating new world to me. Everything I saw, everywhere I went, like a child in her favourite sweet shop, I had a sense of wow and wonder. There was so much to see, so much to learn and so much to adapt to. Papa and my uncles took me, Mummy, Auntie Anna and my younger cousins to see Big Ben and the Houses of Parliament on the River Thames. We walked along the River, seeing St Paul's from a distance and then, from a river cruise, London Bridge and the Tower of London. The stories I heard about these places fired up my imagination and even gave me a sense of having been here before. Some parts of London felt eerily familiar to me. With the sun shining and people smiling, eating ice cream or drinking all kinds of drinks I had never seen before, it seemed to me that London had to be the best city in the world. At Madame Tussaud's, I made a point of learning the names of every single important British person and celebrity I came across.

English, however, posed a problem. I had only ever studied in an English school in India and my teachers in London said that my written English and grammar were at least two years ahead of that of the local children. Spoken English, however, was another matter. At my private school in Porbandar, since we had children from all over India, we spoke mostly in Hindi to each other. When we did speak in English, it was a whole other kind of English, a sort of Hindi hybrid or 'Hinglish', and that too with Gujarati accents and intonations and gesticulating with a spring-bound head and expressive hands. Pronunciations were so different. Saying 'snakes' instead of 'snacks' or 'shempu' instead of 'shampoo' or 'pennying' instead of 'paining' was normal. V's were particularly difficult for our tongue because in most Indian languages, there was no distinction between 'v' and 'w' and the Indian sound fell in between the two, making 'woice' of 'voice' and 'wery' instead of 'very' and 'jweleri' for 'jewellery'.

Sure enough, we used English words but loaded with phrases that were literal translations from our languages, such as saying "Your head!" to dismiss someone with exasperation when in English-English you might say, "Never you mind!" Or in answer to my British teacher's question, "Did you hit Daniella today in the playground, Smita?" I answered, "Yes, she was trying to bully me but," because that was how I would say it in Gujarati.

I once told my teacher, "Miss, sleep is coming. Can I go home?" Words such as 'timepass' for doing something fun to pass the time, commonly littered our spoken Hinglish, or 'funda', short for fundamental but used colloquially when we might not have understood a principle taught in a class. "What 'funda' was Sir telling, *yaar?*" In Hinglish grammar, using 'tell' when in English you would use 'say' and 'listen' when you meant 'hear' was common, as was the overuse of 'would' in place of 'will'. "We would go swimming." We wove in pure Hindi or Gujarati words in an otherwise English sentence. Then of course, our English had quaint residues from the colonial days of the British Raj, using words now antiquated in England, like 'rascal' or 'fellow' or 'thrice'. Teachers regularly asked us to 'do the needful' or called someone a 'duffer' if he was constantly at the bottom of class.

I only realised when I landed at Heathrow Airport that, despite all my English schooling, I had never actually *heard* a British person speak English. The sounds that came out of the mouths of airport officials sounded to me like a pure jumble of gibberish. It was English but not as I knew it. I could understand not a word! And they couldn't understand me with my Gujarati or 'Gujju' Hinglish. How I now wished that I had taken more seriously our Parsi teacher, Rosie Madam, as we called her, who taught us English. She tried painstakingly to demonstrate how certain words were pronounced with a proper English accent. My friends and I thought these bizarre and pompous sounds so hilarious that we couldn't help bursting instantly into fits of giggles. We didn't believe anyone could possibly want to speak in such a hysterically funny way.

How I now regretted making it a source of our daily entertainment, when, for the first six months at least, because of my Hinglish, it was my turn to be made the object of ridicule with the kids at my new school in London. It took me about a year to let go of saying things like, "In class today we discussed about English History," and, "I passed out my exam".

Thanks to the excellent teachers at my primary school, in less than a year I was speaking English with a London accent, "Like a Britisher," as my grandad Motabhai said when I went back to visit him for the first time in Porbandar. I started learning French, too. Before coming to England, I had barely heard of French but within a year, I was like a duck to water with these languages and was consistently getting top marks.

Life at home was a breeze, now that I was again with Grandma Motima and Auntie Anna. Papa's youngest brother, Uncle Nihal, also lived with us. He was my fun uncle with a tremendous sense of humour. I could laugh and joke all I wanted with him, and Motima would not tell us to stop. He bought new vinyl records every Saturday, Soul or Jazz-Funk imports, to which he and I sang at the top of our lungs and danced around the house. Uncle Nihal and Auntie Anna often took me away with their friends on trips to Brussels or Copenhagen or the Lake District, and we went to see English or Hindi films at the cinema. Though they were Papa's youngest brother and sister, being only ten and twelve years older than me, in my heart they were more like my own yearned for brother and sister.

Time flew by in this busy but happy household. I studied for the next four years at an acclaimed girls' secondary school, studying for 'O' levels. Meanwhile, one family at a time, my two eldest uncles and their families were able to move out into their own separate homes. The downside was that my lovely little cousins also went with them, leaving our house quiet as a closed church hall, which took some getting used to.

It wasn't long before my parents, too, were able to move out into a home of their own. I was seventeen and had just started studying for my 'A' levels at a sixth form college. Obvious though it might have been to everyone else, it did not occur to me that I would have to go and live with them. My home had for most of my life been with Grandma Motima and Auntie Anna, now more than ever before. Since the day I had been born, they had been there, more so than my parents, and I couldn't imagine life without them. Even though my parents' new home was only five miles from where we were living, I refused to go with them and continued to live with Grandma Motima.

I cannot imagine how this must have hurt my parents, especially my mum but, even seven years after she had come back from the hospital, I still could not bond with her as my mother. This left Grandma Motima with a dilemma, too. She felt responsible for how attached she had allowed me to become to her. While my own mother was aching to have me with her, Grandma Motima, now older, felt that she deserved a quieter life, having raised nine children. And me.

"Expectations that we have of others,
take away their freedom
to become their real Self,
because they have to
provide what you need.
Otherwise they end up suffering
the consequences of your upset.

Remember this: expectations bind."

# 8

# *Shock*

Motima had tried, futilely, on many occasions to make me go and live with my parents. I dismissed her efforts, flatly refusing to go. I just could not imagine now, at seventeen, to make such a big change. In the seven years that I'd lived with them in London, I had become even closer and more attached to my grandmother, aunt, and Uncle Nihal. I found little in common with my birth mother. The thought of moving away from them now, seemed like swimming the English Channel alone in the peak of a cold, grey winter—almost impossible.

Meanwhile, I was a blossoming into a bubbly, confident, self-expressed and feisty teenager, a handful by anybody's standards and one who, at the same time, was becoming well and truly integrated into the freedom-loving British life and culture. Inevitably, this led to clashes of culture at home, with my Grandma Motima being an elderly woman firmly entrenched in unchallenged traditions of an ancient Hindu Indian culture.

What I considered 'bubbly' and 'self-expressed' occurred to my Motima as mouthy, defiant or combative, and generally she felt I was getting above myself. Being at the height of my teenage hormonal explosion, it was only a matter of time before one of our 'culture clashes' would turn into a fully fledged skirmish. Sure enough, the day arrived when I challenged Motima, in the most harmless and innocent possible way, and this for her was the last straw.

"Meeta is getting too difficult to handle now," I overheard her say, in the next room. She was speaking to a distant uncle, Motima's cousin, who was visiting from an Indian village. There was no one else at home that morning but Grandma Motima, me and this rustic distant uncle.

"What's the issue?" he asked.

"Oh, she's always answering back. She's getting right out of hand! She's becoming a master at *dalil*, firing off arguments and debating things that no one has ever questioned, becoming just like a professional lawyer. She shows no respect, despite all that I've done for her. I don't know how much more I can take."

Why was Grandma Motima talking like this? Why did she feel like that? I felt utterly flabbergasted at what

I was hearing. As far as I was concerned, my world revolved around her. I had no intention to disrespect her nor any inkling that she thought this way about me. I wasn't answering back, but just having a normal conversation. If I don't understand something, should I not question? Or if I don't agree with the way things are done, should I just pretend and agree? Worse still, should I lie? Did she not teach me to be honest?

"Yes, well, after all, who's grandchild is she? That grandad of hers is not famous for nothing! She gets her *azaad* (independent but also pejorative for free-spirited or autarchic) genes from him, no doubt. He's a law unto himself, I can tell you. And that mother of hers! Well, no one has ever managed to control her, have they? Look where all that highfalutin education got her. Why do you continue to take on this headache?"

How dare he refer to me as 'headache'!

He continued to spew out his provincial venom, "She's not your child, is she? Just throw her out. Isn't it time you sent her off to her parents, anyway? How long are you proposing to hold on to this *mathakut*?"

Again, he called me a headache! Could Motima not see what he was doing?

Grandma Motima stayed silent.

He continued. "At your time in life, after all that you've gone through, you deserve to take it easy, not raising *azaadi*, (out of hand), 'gobby' teenagers!" He baited Motima, fanning the flames of my grandmother's anger.

"Who was this man? How dare he stir things up in our household?" I thought, as I eavesdropped on their conversation from the hallway, from the other side of the closed sitting room door.

"Well, I've raised her since the day she was born. I'm the only mother that she's known, really," Motima replied, not giving in to his incitement.

"Yes. And look how she pays you back!" he said. "It's absolutely important that you show her, once and for all, that you are not prepared to tolerate any of this *angreji azaadi bijnez* (liberated English attitudes)! All these *Inglissvingliss sanskars* (English ways) are no good for our *dharma* (culture). If you're not careful, you'll set a precedent, just because you have a soft spot for this one. Before you know it, one grandchild will marry an Englishman, another will leave home and set up on his own. Where will it all end? Before you know it, your family will get so out of hand that you'll have no control over anyone or anything. You must rule with an iron grip, especially in a foreign country."

Who was this snake in the grass, poisoning my beloved Motima's mind against me, making me out to be the worst kind of Indian girl, when he had barely made any attempts to get to know me?

"If not for yourself," he continued, "do it for the sake of your younger grandchildren. Do you want your grandchildren to grow up like this one, and throw out all that our ancestors have worked so hard to preserve? You have to make an example of her."

I wanted to go and confront this intruder and slap him so hard across the face that it would teach him never again to meddle in matters that were none of his business. Besides, what did he know, anyway, about the complexities of growing up between two diametrically opposed cultures as a first or second generation immigrant? All that Motima needed was to be given a different perspective, one that allowed her to see that there was nothing wrong with my behaviour, that who was emerging was a bright, spirited, young woman, learning to integrate and navigate her way in a new world, to be shown that she adored her Motima above all else. Instead of alleviating her frustration and soothing her stressed, confused mind, she had a vat of poison dumped on her by her so-called cousin.

The first term of my second year at college had begun, so shortly after hearing this conversation, I slipped out quietly to catch the bus to make my two afternoon classes of the day.

When I returned home, I noticed a pile of plastic carrier bags stacked outside our front door and wondered what they were doing outside. I rang the doorbell as usual, and Motima answered. "Take all your things. They're all in those bags out there. Your uncle Sai will take you to your parents. You have to go and live with them now."

I laughed, thinking Motima was playing a funny joke on me. She slammed the door shut. Not being able to take what she'd just said seriously, I said, "Come on, Motima, what are you saying? That's not funny! Let me in!" Motima would never do that to me.

"Sai, where are you? Take her to her mother's, now!" Motima's voice came from behind the closed door.

"Motima, at least let me come in and tell me what I'm supposed to have done!" I said.

"No, there's nothing to talk about. I've looked after you long enough! Now it's up to you and your parents," she replied with a steely resolve. "Sai, what's taking you so long? Hurry up and take her!" She shouted at my Uncle Sai, who must have been inside the house.

I knocked on the door again, my stomach wringing with rising panic. "Motima, you can't be serious! You can't just tell me to go immediately like this. At least explain to me what I've done wrong and give me a chance to put it right. Motima, please!"

I begged. I pleaded. But it was no use. Neither would she open the door, nor would she explain my crime.

I waited on the doorstep, panic turning to fear and filling every part of my being, shaken, and sobbing with shock. My worst nightmare was coming true. I was being thrown out, rejected. I was not wanted. And I had nowhere to go. Except that is, to the place that was my last resort, to my parents.

"Motima, what are you doing? What's going on? Let's just all talk about this," I heard Uncle Sai say from the other side of the door.

"Just do as I say," I heard Motima react. She sounded adamant.

"But Motima, I don't understand ...." I heard Uncle Sai begin to question.

"Didn't you hear what I just said? Go! Now!" Motima roared.

Uncle Sai opened the door to come out. It was futile to argue with Motima when she was in this mood. I tried to push through and go in while he was coming out. I still could not accept that Motima would really do this, that she was really serious. Maybe she just wanted to teach me a lesson, and she knew this would shake me up. Maybe this time, I had pushed her, inadvertently, too far with something I said and clearly she was in a rage, but I was certain that I could fix it. I always did. After all, I had never actually been *rude* to her. At least, not as far as I could tell and certainly not outright intentionally. It's true that I challenged her at times, but then, I challenged everybody. That was just the nature of being a teenager, wasn't it? It was what we did! Still, she refused to give way, barricading the door from the inside with all her might.

I was now hysterical. It was just after five o'clock of a September evening and people were starting to pass by, on their way home from work. "Come on, let me take you home," Uncle Sai said softly.

"This *is* my home," I replied through my torment. "I'm not going anywhere." I rooted myself at the doorstep, refusing to leave.

Uncle Sai sighed, then knocked on the door, and shouted, "Motima, come on. This is silly. Let her back in."

"Why haven't you left yet?" came the sharp response from the other side. "Do I have to throw you out now as well, Sai?"

I knocked again and again, calling out, "Motima, I'm sorry. Whatever I'm supposed to have done, I promise I won't do it again! *Please*, just let me back in!"

Uncle Sai went to the car and got in, waiting for me to get in, too. I stayed at the doorstep. After a while, he came back out and sat down beside me on the doorstep. "Come on, Meeta," he said softly. "Let me take you to your parents. You can always come back when Motima's in a better mood."

"What have I done, though? I just don't understand. Can't she at least explain that to me, so that I know where I went wrong?" I said through my sobs.

"I'm sure she will, when she's calmer," he replied. "In the meantime, you must not take to heart anything she says or does when she's in a bad mood. It's probably not even anything to do with you." He put his arm around me to console me.

I would always appreciate Uncle Sai's kindness as we sat on the doorstep of the house that I had come to know as home. In those turbulent moments that would come to shape the person that I would become, his gentleness and affection were droplets of a soothing balm on bleeding burns.

He sat with me in silence on the doorstep until I was ready to move on. I cannot be sure how long it was when I finally accepted that Motima was perfectly serious. Because she'd raised me this far, to my teenager's mind it seemed like she was finally washing her hands of me. That she no longer wanted to look after me.

I was on my own.

Or might as well have been, since that's how living with my parents felt to me. Reluctantly, my eyes swollen with unstoppable tears of heartbreak, my spirit crushed by rejection, and my head as confused as a bee that had lost her way into a barren, flowerless desert, I went with Uncle Sai and a handful of bags containing my belongings.

# 9

## Karmic Full Stop

I went to my parents' house feeling rejected and misunderstood. My mum's face lit up on seeing me arrive home, finally. She was thrilled to see me but, wounded and confused as I was, I couldn't embrace my mum with a smile. Uncle Sai brought my things upstairs and left them for me in the room that my parents had intended to be my bedroom. When Papa arrived home that evening from work, he too was overjoyed to see that I was there for good.

As much as I wanted to receive my parents' affection, over the coming days and weeks, I found myself unable to so, pushing them away, resisting them by putting up a wall of a prickly teenager's rage, a flimsy camouflage for my hurting heart. I loathed myself for lashing out at them for something over which they, and I for that matter, had no control, but felt unable to behave differently.

The very next day after moving in, I went back to Grandma Motima's after college to see if I might be able to talk to her today. I desperately hoped, prayed, that things had calmed down in her mind now and that we could have a chat about it all. But they had not. She remained adamant in her resolve that it was time for me to start living with my parents, and she didn't allow me back in.

Without Motima, my world as I knew it had collapsed. I felt powerless and vulnerable, with nothing to live for. Bereft, I ran all the way back to my parents' house, all of three miles, locked myself up in my room and wept desperately the entire weekend. Papa and my mum didn't know what do say or do to make me feel better. They just repeated, "Don't cry, don't cry," which was about as comforting as a duvet without any filling. The more they tried to help, the more I had the urge to push them away. I didn't understand why, and hated myself for it.

My emotional world felt as though I was tied to four separate horses, which pulled at each of my limbs in four different directions. One limb was tied to my grandmother, one to my parents, one to a part of me over which I had no control, and yet another to a future for which I was not ready.

By Sunday night, on my bed in the dark, I could weep no more. My eyes flickered open and shut in the moments before sleep, and my gaze fell on the statues and pictures of gods and goddesses in the small shrine of my bedroom bookshelf. In that half-awake, half-asleep state, I found myself getting up to swipe them away with one arm when, out of her picture, a kind, smiling Goddess Saraswati came alive. The petals of the white lotus she held in one of her hands opened one by one and released a heavenly fragrance that cleared my head. At the same time, her white swan took on life of its own. Tired, my face burning with salt from my tears, I could no longer resist or fight with my circumstances. In the presence of Saraswati and her brilliant white swan, I felt calmer. "Hello! You have no idea how lovely it is to see you again!"

*"Do you remember that you asked me to come back and remind you if you forgot about that conversation we had when you were a little girl?"* The swan replied.

I remembered its sweet, dulcet tones from all those years ago, that time when I had passed out at Motabhai's house. "What am I going to do now without Grandma Motima? Why am I hurting so much? Why am I not able to be with my parents?" As I fired off these questions, the scent of the lotus wafted in through my nose again, and calmed my anguish some more.

*"Remember I told you about the veils of maya?"* the swan asked. I hesitated as I tried to recollect. That

was a conversation from a very distant past: it had gone to the back of my mind while I had been busy enjoying a carefree, happy time growing up in London in my Grandma Motima's household. But, as the swan reminded me of its original question, the memory came flying back. I nodded.

*"That's what's causing you so much heartache and pain. Maya distorts what is real and what is not. It makes you believe that things and people are the source of your happiness and so you become attached to them. It makes you crave and run after what you can't have, and shun what's right and good for you. This makes you miserable. You see, you crave to belong with your Grandma Motima, and yet your parents have been waiting for their turn with you."* The swan hesitated, so I could absorb what it had said.

"But I know I'm happy with Grandma Motima and I'm miserable with my parents," I said. "That doesn't seem like an illusion–it really is how I feel."

*"Yes, it certainly seems like that's how it is but, as you grow up, you'll realise that life is not only about instant gratification or what makes you feel good in the moment. There is a higher purpose to life, and that's about doing your dharma, doing what life needs you to do. For example, let's say you've become too attached to a person but it might be that your karma with that person has burned out, that it has come*

*to an end. So situations arise where you have to move on to the next phase of your life, but if you cling to something that is no longer appropriate, life has to force you to move on."*

I listened to the swan's counsel and took it to heart. "Why does it feel to me like I still love my Grandma Motima, then? Why do I love being so much with my Auntie Anna and my Uncle Nihal?"

*"Because it's true. You do love them, but it's often easy to mistake attachment, or needing someone, for love. You see, real love is one which listens to the needs of the other person as well—not just your own. Real love trusts in giving the other person the freedom to grow in their own way."*

I listened intently. "Are you saying that I'm holding Grandma Motima back because I want to live with her?" I was horrified. It was the last thing I would have wanted.

*"She has her soul's journey too, as do you. I want you to become a master of listening. This means knowing how much to ask of someone and when to let them go to their higher Self."*

The swan's wise words felt so soothing on my frazzled nerves. "I didn't mean to upset her by holding on to her. I thought she wanted that, too."

"I know, sweet thing. I am teaching you uncommon wisdom. Do not blame yourself. All is as it should be. All is well." The swan's words helped. I felt relieved.

"Does that mean I now have to learn to accept my parents and love them in a different way?" I asked, calmer but still desolate.

"Yes, you have much karma to resolve with them," the swan said.

"It's not fair, and I really don't want to."

"Let me tell you a secret. Most people have no idea that relationships have a higher purpose. Every relationship you will ever have, will eventually lead you to recognising your true essential nature, your true Self." My eyes were wide open as I took in this teaching. "If you look at every relationship from that point of view, you will grow faster and also get the best out of them."

"Really?" I asked, mesmerised. "Why is it so important to recognise your true Self?"

"It's not just important, it's your highest dharma, the ultimate purpose of life: to recognise and be true to your Self."

"But then, why do we have all these relationships and complicated problems in life? Why don't we just get straight to the point and work on accomplishing our highest *dharma*?" I felt baffled.

*"You see, your soul is on a long journey but somehow, it completely forgets the purpose behind making the journey. It changes bodies many times on that journey, and in different places at different times—a lot like someone who has a lot of clothes and keeps changing outfits. Along the way, it meets many other souls who are also all on their own journey. During the course of each journey, sometimes the soul experiences joy in certain relationships, and at other times the experiences are more distressing, or the soul makes choices to do things that are harmful to itself or to others, so accruing difficult karma,"* the swan said in a patient voice.

"Is that why you have to have relationships with people? So that you can put things right? Or learn to do better next time?"

*"Yes, sometimes a jiva-atman, which is your own individual soul, the part of the higher Self that takes birth on earth, comes into a relationship to enjoy a certain harmonious karma that you have built up with someone. At other times, you've come here with an agreement to grow and develop together. Or perhaps, it's to give or teach something to another or to receive teaching yourself. Sometimes, it's to work out*

unresolved issues from previous times. But I'm here to teach you that if you can realise what a particular relationship is about, then you will be better able to be and do what that relationship needs. Therefore, it's important to be vigilant to what expectations you have of another person."

"Are expectations destructive?" I asked. "Have I got too many expectations of Grandma Motima?"

"Expectations that we have of others, take away their freedom to become their real Self, because they have to provide what you need, otherwise they end up suffering the consequences of your upset. Remember this: expectations bind." The swan gave me a steady look.

"But I want people to be free to choose for themselves. I don't want to bind anyone," I said, speaking from my heart.

"Exactly! That I know. That is why I am here. To remind you, like you asked me. I'm here to remind you that it's time to remove one of the veils of maya, of illusion," the swan said.

"How can I do that? And what will happen if I do?"

"With every veil you remove, of something you believe is true and real but is, in fact, just a trick of the soul, an illusion, you will become more freed up to know yourself as you really are, as your innate nature."

"But what exactly *is* that? And why should I care? I just want to have fun!"

*"Ah, very good, sweet one. You see, you are a brilliant, sparkling little diamond, just like me!"* And as the swan said that, its glistening white form transformed into a blinding glint of light coming from a brilliant, sparkling diamond. *"And this is who you are! When you will know yourself as this, the innermost truth of who you are, you will not just have 'fun', but that becomes your innate state. It's like you will be 'fun', in its highest octave."* Silence filled the space as I received this awe-inspiring knowledge.

*"Can you see that? You are a brilliant, sparkling diamond. Everyone is,"* it repeated this, so that I would get it. As it spoke, the sparkling diamond turned back into the form of the swan.

"Am I? It's certainly not how I feel right now," I replied. "So, remind me again. What do I have to do to stop feeling this heartache and pain?" I was willing to go along with any remedy the swan had for me.

*"Take a deep breath, close your eyes and take another slow, deep breath,"* the swan said. *"Now, I want you to place your hand on your heart and pluck the pain, as if it were a rotten apple or mango, and give it to me."*

I did as the swan counselled.

*"Now, imagine that your Grandma Motima is standing in front of you. Imagine that there are several thick cords coming from her body into yours. Can you see them?"*

I nodded when the cords appeared in my inner vision. There were several, going into different parts of my body, one thick one into my navel, another lesser one into the centre of my chest, and several thinner ones into my back and lower belly.

*"I want you to call me every time you come across a new veil of illusion, and ask me to cut the cords for you. But you must do it only with utmost love and kindness, not anger or resentment, otherwise the karmic connection will still linger on and on,"* the swan said.

"But if you cut the cords between me and Motima, does that mean I will never see her again? Will she always hate me?" I asked, worried.

*"No, sweet one, quite the opposite. When people are set free to follow their higher purpose, they feel at peace. Sometimes, this helps to take the relationship to a whole new level of harmony and, sometimes, your work together is done and you see less of them. But either way, both of you are freer and more at peace."*

It dawned on me that the swan's teachings, or should I say, my Inner Diamond's counsel, had completely altered how I saw my situation. "I can see more clearly now. I certainly don't want to bind anyone and keep them from their happiness, especially my Grandma Motima. Please, can you cut the cords that bind me and Grandma, so she can be free to be happy and at peace, and so that I can be free of the pain of being separated from her?" I asked, ready to let go.

The swan moved towards the cords and clasped them, then dissolved them completely. As they disappeared, one by one, into the light that emanated from and surrounded the swan, I glimpsed a little light at the end of my dark tunnel too.

*"Throughout your life, you will keep coming across situations that call you to love others, to appreciate them, but to do so without becoming so attached to them that you cannot see who you truly are,"* the swan said, then turned into the flash of a diamond and disappeared.

I slept deeply that night, and awoke the next morning, wondering if I really had travelled to the realm of heaven this time. My heart felt lighter and my nerves less frazzled. For the first time since the incident, I felt a ray of hope in my heart. I realised that the swan in my dream was a depiction of my higher Self, my Inner

Diamond—a glimpse of which I'd had in front of our home shrine when I was seven. It was the true nature that lurked beneath the person or identity that I knew myself to be.

Several months before I moved in with my parents, Uncle Nihal had bought tickets in advance for us and Auntie Anna to go and see one of our favourite bands, Imagination, in concert at London's Tottenham Court Road. In my wildest imagination, I could never have known that when that day came, we wouldn't be living under the same roof. I made my way into central London, as arranged, to meet up with him before we were due to go into the concert hall. I hadn't seen either him or my aunt since I had moved out, so we arranged to meet an hour before the concert. Uncle Nihal gave me a big hug and we went to a nearby cafe.

He could see I was still upset and made silly jokes to lighten me up. Normally, that would have worked, but today I had too many questions. I could tell he felt awkward and wanted to avoid talking about what had happened with Grandma Motima, but I needed to talk to someone about it.

"Why did she throw me out like that, Kaka?" I asked, referring to him as I did in Gujarati. "What have I done? It's not fair to do that without any explanation, is it?" I felt all the sadness, panic and upset flooding over me once again.

"You haven't done anything wrong, silly," he replied. His whole posture told me he felt awkward.

"It doesn't make sense then. All she had to do was explain to me what she wanted and I would have done it," I said.

"But that's just it. You see, I think she did try to get you to understand that she had done everything she could for you and, now that your parents were in a situation to set up home and take care of you. It was high time you three lived together as a family once again."

"But it's too late, don't you think? I'm almost ready for university and I'll be gone in a year from now. Couldn't I just have carried on living with you all for another year or so?"

"You could. But after all that your parents have gone through, how do you think it feels for them to have you continue to live away? They want you with them too," my uncle said.

"Why didn't Motima just explain that to me? I'm not some wildling. I'm sure I would've listened in the end."

"Ah, but I think in her own way, she did try to get you to understand that. Attached as you were to her, do you think you would've listened?" Uncle Nihal asked.

"I would have. Just a bit more patience maybe?"

"From what I saw, I think given a choice, you would have found it hard to make that move. Just consider that Motima did it the only way she felt she could. I think she realised how important it was, especially for your mum."

"But why not let me into the house? Why did she have make it so hard?" I searched for an answer to help me understand further.

"See, you're looking at it only from your perspective, but there are as many sides to the story as there are people involved. So, consider that she wasn't slamming the door on you, but rather on herself. Do you think, given that she's raised you more or less from the day you were born, given how close the two of you have been, that if she'd seen your sweet face, she would have been able to let you go? She was struggling with herself, you see. It was more about forcing herself to do the right thing in the only way felt she could," my uncle said. As he explained, I was in tears all over again, this time from seeing the other side of the coin.

"I can see what you're saying," I said thoughtfully, softened.

"It's just a difficult situation for you and for her, not to mention for your parents," he said. "Let me ask you this, and I want you to answer honestly. If she had said that it was time for your to move in with your parents, would you have gone willingly?"

I considered the scenario for a moment. "Maybe not. But it still doesn't have to be like this. None of this is my fault, is it? I had no choice in who raised me and where I lived. Wherever they put me, I did my utmost to be the best I knew how to be."

"No one is saying any of this is your fault. The reality is, neither of you would be feeling as upset as you are if you didn't love each other to bits. Can you see that?"

"I suppose so. Yes." I could see he had a point. It helped to have had the conversation with Uncle Nihal, though it didn't take away how I felt, nor the impact of the changes I now had to face. It was the first and only time I was able to talk to someone about this, and it helped to have Uncle Nihal share things from Grandma Motima's point of view. It didn't change the situation but, somehow, it helped to include—understand (perhaps better)—how it may have been from my Grandma Motima's perspective and not just my own, and especially, to understand how she had made her decision coming from a place of love and not anger.

As the weeks and months wore on, I allowed the counsel of my Inner Diamond to sink in: our *karma*, that between me and my beloved Grandma Motima, my second mother, had come to a complete and full stop that day.

It was time to be brave and move forward, and embrace the new era that beckoned compellingly.

# 10

## *Indian Summer*

Now life was very different. With just three of us, home somehow felt empty. I had grown used to being in a vibrant house, teaming with people. Until now, Anna and Nihal might well have been my aunt and uncle, and I may have had an extended family full of cousins, but in my world, they were my brothers and sisters, no less.

I remembered that when we were in India and later in London, on the occasions that I dared to whine to Grandma Motima that I didn't have any brothers or sisters, she wouldn't hesitate to scold me. "Don't ever say that! You have many brothers and sisters. That's what all these kids are!" She was referring to my cousins.

"But Motima, can you also tell them the same thing, please, because I don't think they know that," I would reply, being a smarty pants. Only now, it was hitting home that I was, after all, an only child. *I was on my own* and it was for the best that I stopped resisting this simple fact. It would take me some years to come to terms with it but, when I fully accepted it, I realised what a boon this was.

The sudden changes I was forced to face had hit me hard. My parents still felt like strangers, and it seemed like my safety net had been abruptly yanked from beneath me. I no longer felt anchored or grounded, and this stirred up all kinds of insecurities within. My zest for my studies waned, as I was unable to control the uncertainty and upset that overwhelmed me when I woke up each morning, and made my stomach churn with dread. I tried talking to one or two of my close friends about what was troubling me, but no one seemed to understand, or be able to respond in any way that helped me, making me feel even more lost and alone.

Until now, though I was eighteen, I hadn't been interested enough in boys to have already had a boyfriend. More importantly, having such relationships were expressly forbidden in my culture and it wasn't in my nature to hide something so significant from my family. Now that I was eighteen and at college, it became normal to be asked out on dates. So far, I hadn't gone on a single one, but the sense of loneliness got the better of me and I allowed myself to develop a friendship with one particular boy. We went to the cinema often, and I went to parties with the friends in his group, as was the normal thing to do, and before long, we were in a fledgling and somewhat 'young' relationship.

In the whole of the Indian culture, including the ideal portrayed over and over again in Bollywood movies, the epitome of a good Indian girl was to have one love and one love only. To sacrifice herself, if necessary, to not marry or love another if things didn't work out with her first love—the ultimate love of her life. For the entirety of life. I, too, wished this ideal to be so for me, but it was a matter of just months when my first boyfriend, so-called, betrayed himself to be a prize jerk, when I heard rumours that he was seeing other girls. This left me feeling more alone and lonely than when I had met him. I decided I wasn't yet ready to embark on boyfriend-girlfriend relationships, and concentrated on my studies.

After my 'A' levels, which I passed that summer, my head was still in a fog and now, without the structure of my studies, I felt more lost than ever, especially when it came to choosing what to study at university. There was no one whose advice I could seek when it came to furthering my academic education. My parents, who had never studied in the UK and who were still getting used to living here, had no idea of how the system worked, and I didn't know who else to turn to.

So while I figured out what I wanted to study for a degree, I put in full-time hours in the job at the central London store where I had been working for the last few years at weekends and holidays. When college opened for the new school year in September, I enrolled into the computing course, fully intending to only stay for one year while I applied for my degree course at university. However, in November, Grandad Motabhai sent a telegram to Papa, saying that his health had taken a turn for the worse and could Papa send me and my mum to visit him. It sounded urgent, so Papa made the arrangements for me and mum to leave within days.

It was our very first visit back to India, eight years after we had left. We landed at Bombay Airport, with its humid thirty-two degree heat and not-so-organised chaos, its friendly people and manic, beeping traffic, and I felt instantly at home. Now I had not one, but two, outstanding places to call home. The family friends, with whom we were going to stay, lived in one of the nicest parts of Bombay, right on the coast of the Arabian Sea. My family had known this family for several generations, and they were about as warm and welcoming as Indian families could be. Their boys were in my age group and we had known each other since birth, with many a water fight that had cemented our friendship.

Only now, we were all older. As I stayed there for a few days, before moving on to my grandad's in Porbandar, our friendship flourished, especially with one of them, Arjun. We got on like a house on fire.

Being avid readers of books of all kinds and having a similar sense of humour, we really enjoyed each other's company. Over the coming weeks and months, we stayed in touch by phone and our friendship continued to blossom, betraying flashes of potential for a young romance.

We stayed with my Grandad Motabhai, and travelled around with my mum, her sister, and her family, in Rajasthan, and along the Arabian Sea coast of Gujarat, in an area called Saurashtra. When I returned to Bombay, five months later, Arjun's family had arranged for us all to go to Mahabaleshwar, a hill station in the Western Ghats of Maharashtra, a beautiful, evergreen forest region. It was an area that had been frequented regularly by the nobility of the British Raj to escape into cooler climes from the arid Indian summers.

I was in full holiday swing and in my element, a million miles from my troubles, and mixed in like a native with everyone I had met on my holidays. From the Bombay boys, who only spoke in English with a sing-song Bombay accent, to my relatives in the villages living the rustic lifestyle, I was discovering myself. Everything looked rosy from where I stood, here in the relaxed atmosphere of India, still before its economic explosion. Our ancient values of family, friendship, and respect for an age-old cultural tradition still thrived. So too did an appreciation for a good sense of humour. My friendship with Arjun developed overtones of a tender and innocent *amour*, not the fast and furious, Western kind, which evaporated into instant gratification, but the gentle Indian sort, slowly simmering, full of possibility, and promising a beautiful future.

Towards the end of my travels in India, I spent my last days in Bombay, staying with Arjun and his family. One day, quite out of the blue, Arjun's mum, watching us falling about laughing over some silly joke, asked him, "Wouldn't you like to get engaged to Smita?" I nearly fell off the sofa. In my mind, this had not been part of the natural course of events—certainly not so soon—not at all. And yet, this was not atypical of how things worked in our culture. Arjun nodded shyly. And that was it. Who was I to say otherwise? Things were settled without me saying a word.

At the same time, the teenager in me, feeling flattered, felt blown away with happiness. I loved these people and it seemed they liked me. The lifestyle of Bombay was enjoyable. There were so many possibilities for me here, including continuing with my studies. Arjun's mother spoke to Papa and Grandad Bapuji in London, and Grandad Motabhai in Porbandar, and agreed to join the two of us at a future date in a respectable manner. It seemed everybody saw a beautiful couple, sweethearts, in a budding Bollywood romance.

I later learned that some of the elders in our family had held a secret wish for the two of us to come together in marriage since we were born, but it was not openly discussed, probably so as not to frighten or drive us away. Perhaps, it was also to give us the illusion that somehow, we had chosen each other of our own accord. Everybody thought that their long-standing wish was coming true and tried not to gloat too much. This would almost have been true, had it not been for one fact—that I was far from ready.

Only, that realisation had yet to dawn on me.

My time together with Grandad Motabhai had been a godsend for both of us. His health recovered and was restored to normal. I, meanwhile, left India a different person to the one that had landed there six months before, having undergone nothing short of a natural healing from my recent anguish. Grandad Motabhai held me in such affection and high regard, that it was impossible not to see myself from his view. Being with him over the last months, my confidence and inner strength were not just restored, but it also opened a window into seeing a bigger possibility of who I could become. This was because in character, I was a reflection of him in so many ways. A formidable and self-made man, he held a mirror for me as to who I could be.

The fun and laughter in my unexpected, nascent romance had also served to heal. Though I didn't know it yet, it had placed me on a stepping stone to something within me that would eventually become the making of me.

In a short space of time, Arjun and I had become close. With me back in London and him still in Bombay, we missed each other like lovesick puppies. It was as if I had left one of my arms behind in Bombay. We wrote letters to each other almost every day. We called each other way more than our parents could afford, lumbering them with international phone bills that were higher than the cost of our flights, which in the early eighties, were expensive.

# 11

## Back to Reality

Over the next year, I carried on working. The company I had been working with persuaded me to undergo management training and gave me a large shop of my own to run. I was just nineteen years old, generating a revenue stream of hundreds of thousands of pounds in business, managing more than twenty people, all of whom were older than me, and I was enjoying every moment of it. I would find that within less than eighteen months, this challenge would become too small and I would go searching for a much larger one, but for now, I was lapping up every bit of learning I could about running a retail business in London.

As the months went by, I still missed Arjun but I had also made a fresh start for myself in London. I had begun to wake up to the fact that there were so many things I wanted to do and accomplish. I wanted, for example, to see the world and learn about its different peoples and their cultures. I wanted to excel in business and work internationally. The areas in which I faced limitations also illuminated themselves as I made baby steps on my own into the adult world. It became clear to me how much I still had to learn about life, and resolve emotionally in myself.

After finishing my 'A' levels, though, I had difficulty figuring out which direction to focus my studies at university, as a yearning had been slowly brewing in the background. I wanted to make something of myself in my life, with my own efforts. A sense that I had a lot to offer had emerged in the last months, all beneath the surface of my mind. Seeds of what I was capable of achieving if I applied myself had been germinating all of their own accord beneath my conscious awareness. Green shoots of aspirations and of a thirst for living life to the full had begun to push through.

There was so much I wanted to do, see and discover. I realised too, that as much as I enjoyed Bombay and India, I absolutely loved living in London. Its hustle and bustle were mere whispers of a city that vibrated with exciting potential. It was a unique, thriving place, full of opportunity. So much was possible here.

In the background, preparations were being made quietly by our families. One evening, I came home from work and overheard the elders talking to my parents. One of them asked Papa, "Smita'll be twenty soon. It's time she was married. The Ravals have been chasing us to set the wedding date. They're keen for the marriage to go ahead soon. They're saying as early as in three months. They're a great family and we shouldn't mess them around. What do you say, Raju? Shall we confirm the date they're asking for?"

As I overheard them talking, I was perturbed to realise that I was filled with dread at the thought of being married off so soon. It made me claustrophobic. I left the house and went for a long, long walk. I didn't understand my feelings. Arjun was a fantastic guy and I was more than sweet on him. We got on so well together. And yet, now ... now that they wanted me to get married, *in few months*, all I wanted to do was to just run and run, away from the whole thing. Why did I feel this way?

I carried on as if I had heard nothing, hoping that the dread and resistance would simply evaporate. After all, I had really enjoyed my time in India and I could see a future there, with Arjun. It wasn't as if I had stopped having feelings for him. And yet, troubling doubts grew by the day. The next evening, Papa called me into the living room to talk about the conversation he had had with the elders the day before. "We've been in conversation with the Ravals. They're keen to set the date for the wedding ..."

"Sorry, Papa," I said, running out the door. "I have to go drop off something to a friend's. I'll be back late.

Can we talk about it tomorrow?" Then the next day, "Papa, I think I forgot my credit card at the petrol station. I'd better go and see if it's still there. Can we talk about this later?" And I ran off the following day. I made some other excuse and the day after that, yet another. Day after day, I avoided Papa until he realised that something was definitely wrong.

Two weeks went by like this. On Sunday, at lunchtime, he called me into the living room and, before I could slip away again, he shouted with a thundering voice, "Sit down!"

I wouldn't be able to get away today. "I need to talk to you. Are you avoiding talking about the wedding? We have to answer to Arjun's family about the wedding date."

Every fibre of my being wanted to run out of that door. Neither could I answer in the way Papa wanted, nor was I able to escape. I felt trapped.

I finally erupted like a pressure cooker. "I'm not ready, Papa!" I screamed. "I need time!"

"What do you mean, you need time? You've had nothing but time. How much time do you need? A day, two days? I thought you wanted to be with Arjun as soon as possible? I mean, you're always writing to each other and talking on the phone to him. I don't understand," he said, alarmed.

"I know. But I didn't realise ... I didn't know ... I thought I would be okay with this ... I'm too young ... Oh, I don't know why. I can't explain!" I struggled to collect my thoughts. I felt as scared as a hounded hare and I didn't expect Papa to understand.

"You're being daft now. We can't keep them waiting. They've been patient enough. Do you realise what a special family they are? What a fantastic, honourable young man Arjun is? You'll not find another guy like him in a hurry, if ever." Papa spoke to me in reasonable tones, although he sounded really worried and flipped out.

Increasingly exasperated, he said, "You can't expect me to go and tell them that. It's not our way." I could see Papa didn't know how to handle the situation. "It's a matter of our family honour, our reputation in the community. It's not our way to chop and change our minds at whim. Our word means something. It has value. We are Brahmins. Our word is our bond. This is not child's play." Papa was properly panicked.

I stayed silent, eyes cast to the floor. I was confused with all the turmoil I felt within me, but I tried to find some rationale that I could give Papa. He deserved that, but I felt so torn in myself. I wanted to be that good Indian girl, I did, and I could see that if I didn't go through with this, the consequences would be grave and far-reaching. The elders would not be half as understanding as Papa.

Even knowing that, something deep within me awakened, something that felt real, and it was compelling and urgent. I heard faint whispers of a profound, calm part of me that I'd rarely glimpsed before, and I couldn't switch it off.

"What do you expect me to tell everyone?" Papa asked, perturbed.

"I don't know, Papa. Can't you tell them I'm not ready, that I need more time?"

"I can't do that, Meeta. It doesn't work like that. Why are you saying all this now? Everything was fine."

"But I'm just not ready ..."

Papa tried to reassure me. "Nobody is ever ready. You will be fine."

"No, no. This is different. Please try to understand." I was about to melt into tears.

"Look, why don't you take a few days to think this over. Let's talk again mid-week," Papa offered, seeing me dispirited and cheerless. It wasn't my father's way to be forceful. He was man of spiritual values. He valued freedom and, ultimately, it mattered more to him to act with integrity than to pander to appearances and other people's opinion. Above all, my happiness mattered to him. He also knew well how headstrong I could be once I had made up my mind about something.

I felt hemmed in and trapped. I hated having so many people involved in what I felt was, after all, my life. I felt exposed and vulnerable with so many people having an opinion about something that was so private to me. I needed to be given the space to work out what was right for me. I had met a nice, good-looking lad and we had got on well. It was an exquisite experience and I wanted to be that virtuous *desi nari*, that good Indian girl who sheepishly went off, married her first love and lived happily ever after with a litter of children. But I was barely twenty and I had no clue about who I was.

The last thing I had intended was to put Papa in this difficult position, and I felt awful for doing just that. I needed to get out of the house and think. I needed someone to talk to, someone who could see things from my perspective, who could help me untangle the many threads of realisation, aspiration, wishes, hopes, and awakening that were happening within me all at once. It had to be someone mature, who had the ability to see things objectively, someone with guts to not succumb to cultural pressure. Was there anyone who could mediate on my behalf with the family? Who could I turn to? No one came to mind, except my friend Gina.

I had become friends with her some years before when I was working part-time as a Saturday girl in a London store. Over the past couple of years, we had become good friends. We had a good laugh and enjoyed going out together after work, and lately I had been spending more and more time at her house. She was studying for her masters degree, but worked part-time at the same place as me to help pay for her studies. Being older than me, she was the only one whom I could talk to about the difficult situation I found myself in. I could always pour my heart out to her, and she had been very helpful in supporting me over the last few weeks, but this particular weekend she was away in Paris.

This was all too real. The thought of being married off filled me with dread and heaviness. I hadn't expected to feel this way. It was not supposed do be like this.

I had to figure out what was going on with me and I had to do it fast. Frankly, this upsurge of resistance was new to me, too. Things were surfacing within that were not part of my conscious thinking. Where was all this coming from?

Not knowing where to go and who to talk to, I took my bewilderment with me and got into my little brown Mini Cooper, which I had proudly bought with a bank loan of one thousand pounds, a small fortune in those days. I found my way west onto the M40, going towards Oxford. The afternoon sun of England's summer poured through the glass, making me sweat even more than I already was. I opened the front windows to let the breeze cool me, and kept driving until Marlow, where I came off and took the road past the town centre, towards Henley. Along the way, a mile or two away from the town centre, I had previously discovered a turn off that led all the way to the edge of the River Thames. Sometimes, in the summer when I fancied being in the open countryside, I went there for a walk with a friend. It was beautiful and peaceful, and often you would hardly encounter a soul, other than the mallards, grebes, cormorants and white swans that frolicked on the river's surface, and maybe the odd canal barge or river boat moored at the river's side.

With an old newspaper that I had lying around in the boot of my Mini and a notebook that I carried around in which I wrote my daily journal—something I had started to do when I was fourteen—I headed to find a solitary spot along the riverside. Sure enough, there was no one about and a little way along the river's verge, I laid down the newspaper and sat on it.

"What am I going to do now?" I asked myself quietly, my mind whirling with upheaval and fear. I stared at two beautiful white swans that swam together in concert. It is said that swans mate for life. I wondered how they knew which swan was the right one for them. It was a question of *life*, after all.

In my notebook, I started to scribble my confused thoughts. Often, the process of jotting down the things that had happened in my day, or writing about feelings and emotions, good or challenging, helped to straighten my mind. It was like untangling a ball of wool that had entwined itself into countless little knots. The positive things became more grounded and amplified, and I was able to make sense of the things I found more difficult.

"Inner Diamond, I need your help. Please talk to me," I jotted down. "I urgently need to get clear about why I am so confused about my life. What must I do now?" I looked around me, feeling utterly lost and terrified about my situation.

"Everyone expects me to get married," I carried on scrawling. "I liked the notion of it, but now that they're talking about actually setting a date for the wedding, it's freaking me out. I just don't feel ready. I'm too young! Just twenty. It's too soon. What do I know about life? I want to be a good wife. I want to be devoted to my husband, like a well-bred Indian woman is meant to be. But how can I do that when I don't have the first clue about my own self, my own nature? I get so angry and frustrated at times and I can't control those feelings. I hate that about myself. How can I live inside a big family when, at the drop of a hat, without much provocation, I can completely lose my temper? How is flying off the handle like that going to go down in my new family? They think so well of me now. It's just a matter of time before I go and ruin that impression, before they see how immature and awful I really am."

I looked up and saw a brilliant blue kingfisher dive in and pluck out a small, plump fish from beneath the surface of the river. A sudden sharp twinge of envy shot up through me, pinching at my heart as I watched the kingfisher flying about in absolute freedom. "How I wish I could be free!" As I wrote these words, the familiar feeling that had been silently arising within me over the last few months, spread throughout my being and enveloped me.

"What *is* this feeling that's been welling up slowly but so strongly over the last few months?" I wrote. "It's niggling me now. It's *that* feeling that's causing me to be so confused." A pair of mallards glided gracefully onto the water from full flight. They landed and then disappeared, diving deep into the river, probably to search for some food for nourishment. Their diving deep, somehow, helped me to get in touch with what I myself was searching for, and a new realisation swam into my consciousness. "Ah! This feeling, it's not just a feeling but a longing. It's a longing from deep within my soul. Some deep part of me yearns to be free, like the kingfisher."

I felt a sense of instant relief as this sensation, which had been niggling and gnawing at me, finally clicked into place in my understanding. I felt a flash of momentary elation.

"But what does that mean?" I wrote. "It's not as if anyone is physically shackling me. Why do I feel this yearning to be free? I mean, my parents don't stop me from going out or seeing my friends or doing anything that I have so far wanted to do. Doesn't that mean that I *am* free?"

It was then I heard that faint inner voice. It wasn't the sound of my own thoughts. It was very different. It had a quality of something other: still, clear and pure. Though it was new to me, it felt somehow familiar. I let my hand move across the page to write what I was 'hearing', not just through my inner ears but through my intuitive senses. It was my Inner Diamond, the one that Saraswati's swan had shown me a few days ago.

*"You are asking the wrong question. The question you should be asking is another one,"* the Inner Diamond said. I was aghast with surprise and delight all at once. I had never before summoned up my Inner Diamond in this way. Never had I experienced such a clear connection or direct communication with it in such a straightforward manner. Not wanting to break this connection, I continued writing and engaging with it in this extraordinary way.

"Please tell me, what is that question?" I wrote.

*"It's a question that for most, takes many lifetimes to answer,"* the Diamond said. *"The real question your soul longs for you to answer in this lifetime is: How can I experience the essence of Who I Am?"*

"My mum and dad always tell me that I'm this or that. Am I not listening to them? Should I listen better next time?" I asked, not quite understanding what the swan was telling me.

"Your parents love you very much and what they tell you is valuable. But you need to look beyond what people say about you and even what you believe about yourself. Look beyond the superficial veil of maya. Do not define yourself through others, how they see you and how they expect you to behave. Do not even define yourself merely through your likes and dislikes of everyday things. You are much deeper and richer than that. Discover that about yourself, and then you will be happier. Then, the choices you make and the things you do will be more fulfilling."

"But is it not all too selfish? Am I not just being selfish if I just go after what I want?"

"This is the great human misunderstanding. There is nothing selfish about discovering the Self. Indeed, that is the ultimate purpose of life," the Inner Diamond said. "Once you truly know your Self, you are more free to serve others without the veils of maya. You are less attached to the things that do not matter. You experience the boundless Self."

I knew nothing about the ultimate purpose of life, nor about who I was. What was becoming abundantly clear, was that I had a whole life to live before I would be ready to be the kind of partner that I wanted to be to anyone. Being anything less just didn't seem worthwhile.

I closed my eyes and took a sharp intake of breath, relieving the tightness and fear trapped in my chest. Like pieces of a movie, glimpses of an older woman flashed behind my closed eyes. I was struck by how at ease and at home in her skin this woman looked—such a contrast to me. She looked young, but her demeanour was that of someone accomplished and 'well travelled', not just in the ways of the world but in the inner realms, as if she knew something of her real Self. She smiled and laughed, enjoying the material fruits of her hard-earned labour, but the bright glow she exuded seemed to come from a deeper place in her being. Did it come from being at peace within herself? She looked settled, as if all was well in her world and she wanted for nothing.

A man sat by her side. He, too, was older. The two of them were as comfortable with each other as if they had been together for aeons. I couldn't help noticing something of an aura or enigma about both of them, individually and together. Although I couldn't see what this thing was, it inspired me. These glimpses I was being shown, contained something special. Like a magnet pulling me into my own future, they seemed to be drawing me towards them. A few moments later, I opened my eyes and let everything I'd just seen sink in.

Just then, the pair of lover swans circled back towards the edge of the river where I was sitting and, quite unexpectedly, a cygnet emerged from beneath the wings of the mother swan, and swam alongside its parents. Then, from underneath the other wing, another cygnet showed itself and frantically swam over to join its little sibling, then tried to take over its lead. I gasped at the marvellous beauty of what I had just witnessed. I would, perhaps, one day like to have a family of my own. Unlike the mother swan, however, I was a long way from being capable of being either a good partner or the rock-solid mother that I would wish to be.

It struck me that what I was being shown was that I had to discover myself both as who I was within but also, who I could be in the world. I realised, so clearly now, that I first needed to make it on my own. I needed to have a successful career so that I could understand what I was capable of and what my natural talents were. I needed to stand on my own two feet and be responsible for making my life happen. Only then, could I begin to know how to win at the challenges of life with maturity.

Goosepimples covered my arms as I saw a vision of buying my own place to live in, my sanctuary, from which to discover and develop myself. This clear vision inspired me to become the kind of person of whom I could be proud, someone who could be of service in the world.

Sitting on the edge of the River Thames that afternoon, I realised what an important turning point I had reached in my young life, and how significant the choice that I was about to make would prove to be in shaping the person I would become.

As I drove back home, I felt excitement initially, but it wasn't long before fear and dread emerged. How on earth was I going to explain all this to Papa? Worse still, how would he explain it to Grandad Bapuji? The sheer terror that thinking about this brought up, made me want to abandon the idealistic longings and vision I had just had. This was all just a big dream. Never in a million years was I going to be allowed to step back from going through with the engagement and marriage.

Sweat broke out on my forehead and chest. "What shall I do?" I found myself saying out loud, fearful. No sooner had I said the words, than the answer came from my Inner Diamond.

*Have the courage to trust your Self.*

"Fear of the unknown
paralyses people.
Become a master of
flowing with uncertainty."

# 12

## *Courage of Conviction*

Darkness had settled in by the time I arrived home. By the riverside, it had seemed like I had been in a time bubble. Mum had cooked some of my favourite things, including Gujarati *handvo*, a baked dish of ground rice and shredded, spiced vegetables such as carrots, courgettes, *dudhi* (a white Indian squash with a light green skin and white flesh). She made it beautifully, with a sesame crusted, crisped upper layer. I would normally not have been able to resist this speciality but, this evening, the thought of having to tell Papa that I would definitely not be getting married killed my appetite.

My dad was sitting in the lounge. "Papa, can I talk to you?" I asked timid and brave, all at once. I had never needed to dig so deep within myself as today to find my reserves of courage.

"Yes, *beta*. Tell me," he replied calmly. But I could see he was hiding his nervousness. I looked at his drained face and realised that he had been worried sick for days about what I was going to do.

"Papa, I've been thinking, trying to get clear about why I feel the way I do," I said, edgy at the thought of how he might react.

"Yes? And what have you decided?" he asked.

"Papa, I'm really, really sorry to do this to you, and to the family, and to Arjun's family. I'm just not ready yet. I really want to grow and learn and become a better person before I can take such a massive step as marriage." Tears welled up as my words left me. "I'm so sorry, Papa."

"But, I just don't understand. I thought you two got on so well? I thought you were so sweet on each other, writing and calling all the time. What was all that about? What's changed?"

"It is just like you say. And it never occurred to me that I might not be ready for it. Something inside me just keeps telling me that I must grow up first, and that I must learn to stand on my own two feet before I do anything so big as marriage and kids."

"But people as young as you get married all the time and they figure things out along the way. You may never find someone as kind and smart and generous and as well bred as Arjun again, *beta*. Guys like him come along maybe once in a lifetime, if you're lucky," Papa said. I could feel his heart crumbling.

"Papa, I know, I know—"

"What, 'you know'? You know nothing," he said in an angry tone.

"That's exactly what I'm saying—I don't know anything, Papa."

"That's why you should trust us, your parents. We do know what's right for you. After all, we want you to be happy." His words were sharp.

"But, Papa, please trust me—"

"How can I trust you? One day you're all happy, and the next you change your mind, like the wind. You have no idea what you're saying. The impact of this may be something you will never be able to live down." His eyes scoured my face. "And what do you expect me to tell your Grandad Bapuji? Even if I understand, he's from a different generation. He won't be happy about this at all. Our family name is at stake here."

I felt a glimmer of hope at his words, because they showed he was beginning to deal with the difficult challenge of telling others about this turn of events. "I might be making the biggest mistake of my life, Papa, but I know deep down it's what I need to do. I promise I won't disappoint you. Please, tell me you'll support me with this." I went over and threw my arms around him, begging, pleading and weeping. "I've never asked you for anything before, have I, Papa? And I won't again. Please, please don't make me do something when I know it's just not my time yet."

Papa, as hard as he had decided to be on this matter, melted. I was in genuine distress, and when all was said and done, I was making a difficult but authentic choice that in my heart of hearts I believed in.

He gave a heavy sigh. "Are you absolutely sure about this?"

I nodded.

"Well, I'll call Arjun's mother and explain to her—though I have no idea how to ... It's too late now to call India, but I'll do it tomorrow morning, before I leave for work."

"No, no, please don't tell her yet. I'd rather speak to Arjun myself, first. I don't want him to hear it from anyone else. Please let me speak to him first."

"Okay. But no more lingering. Call him first thing in the morning, yes?" he replied.

"I will, Papa. I'm really, very sorry to put you in this position. I'm so sorry," I said. Then I ran to my room and threw myself on my bed, loathing myself for shattering so many people's hopes and hearts.

"Throughout your life,
you will keep coming across
situations that call you to
love others, to appreciate them,
but to do so without becoming
so attached to them that you
cannot see who you truly are."

# 13

## The Phone Box

All night, I tossed and turned, sleep eluding me, as the prospect of talking to Arjun loomed large. Determined as I was to tell him the truth, I could not bear the thought of hurting him. After all, the only thing he had done was brighten up my life. He had brought sunshine at a time when I was down in the dumps, still in pain. How nasty was I to then reward him with such hurt? He did not deserve this. He wanted nothing more than us being together, being happy. Was this absolutely necessary? Was there another way? Maybe he would wait for me? But would that be fair on him? These and many other questions went round and round and round again in my mind, and yet I was determined, more than ever, to take responsibility for driving my life according to my inner call.

At five o'clock in the morning, I gave up trying to sleep and got out of bed, showered, and dressed for work. I decided to leave the house early so I could call Arjun from a phone box. That way, I wouldn't wake up my parents, and I also wanted to be able to talk to him without them overhearing. India was four and a half hours ahead of British Summer Time and I wanted to catch Arjun just before his lunchtime. The tube station was just five minutes from my house, but today I drove to a station much further away, as I didn't want to bump into anyone I knew in my local area. Along the way, I stopped at a petrol station to get coins in exchange for a wad of sterling pound notes for the phone. Calls to India were expensive and I wanted to be able to talk to Arjun for as long as the conversation would take.

At the tube station, I parked my car and went to the red phone box just outside, but there was someone already in there. Meanwhile, dark thunderous clouds had let rip and it poured down with rain, with occasional gusts of wind. I waited outside the phone box, getting wet, as the person inside looked like he might not take too long. He once put the phone down and I thought he was about to come out but he stayed on to make another call.

As I waited in the rain, my mind raced wild. What would I tell him? I loved him so much. I didn't want to hurt him. I hadn't spoken to Arjun for a few weeks now. Every time he called, I was out, either still at work or I had gone somewhere. I'd stayed out more than usual, to avoid having Papa confront me to talk about this situation. A part of me wanted to share with Arjun what I was dealing with, because I had got into the habit of telling him everything, but another part didn't dare to.

How I wished Gina was here. But ultimately, I had to make my choices for myself, on my own. I felt miserable and very alone, in the gushing rain.

What would he say? Would he understand? Would he be heartbroken? Was I a bad person for doing this? Would he hate me forever for it? My hair was now drenched and so was my face, as I stood and thought about the pain I was about to inflict on an innocent boy who had done nothing whatsoever to harm me. Would I be able to tell him? Suddenly, I was filled with self-doubt. Was I doing the right thing? Was I just being selfish? Once again, fear and dread held me in their clutches. My heart thumped like a panicked, caged animal. I had to get out. I had to be free. These thoughts raced in my mind, all of their own accord, and made my knees wobbly and weak.

Was there something wrong with me? Was I not capable of being loved? Did I have what it took to be loved? Was I just scared, like Papa said? Maybe I was just scared, terrified even, of being loved. Was I not now doing to him and his lovely family what I myself I had experienced? Was I so stupid that because of my selfish and immature behaviour, I was pushing away a guy who was so perfect for me? Would I ever find someone as wonderful as him? Tears of frustrated helplessness and sadness gushed down my face at the thought of the cruel deed of fate I was about to commit. Young as I was, I could not turn back on so compelling a call and yet, I felt devastated. I questioned myself: Could something that was so hard and possibly wrong to do, in reality, be so right?

It seemed that I stood at the edge of a cliff, about to take a leap of faith. Was I completely misguided? Would I crash and burn? I felt like I was close to wetting my pants with fear, my knees still wobbly and weak, as I looked into the phone box, impatient for the man to come out. These two or three minutes seemed like the longest of my life. What was this man doing in there? Could he not see that I needed to have the most difficult conversation of my life with the guy I loved? What was taking him so long? Then, he finally hung up the phone and I rushed in, pushing the drenched hair off my face and wiping my tears with the back of my hand, only to find it streaked with running black mascara from my eyes.

I got a fistful of coins out of their small plastic bags, and clumsily pushed in a series of coins as I began dialling Arjun's number. A few coins slipped from my wet hand onto the floor. I bent down to pick them up and as I did so, a few more slid out from my other hand. Frustrated and in a raging panic, I tried to calm myself down and start dialling the number all over again. The rain pelted down relentlessly. I could hear the phone ringing at the other end. One ring, second ring ... my heart thumped hard and loud. I feared it might just jump out into the phone box. On the third ring, I was relieved to hear Arjun answer.

"Hello?" I could hear in his voice the hope that it would be me at the other end.

I couldn't have feigned a pleasant conversation about the weather with any one of his family members today. "Hi, it's me ..."

"Hi, you! I was worried about you. Why haven't you returned my calls? It's been weeks since we've spoken. I've missed you. Are you okay?" he asked. Happiness and concern were both evident in his voice. Something in his tone betrayed that somehow, he sensed something was up. It wouldn't be altogether unusual, as we did experience a telepathic connection between us at times. "You're not avoiding me, are you?"

"Ummmmm ... ummmmm ...," I struggled. I just had to say it as it was, "Arjun, there's something I need to talk to you about."

The line went terribly silent. "Hello? Hello? Arjun, are you there?" Then, at the other end of the phone, coming from what must have been an open window, I heard the loud roar of thunder and a downpour of loud, monsoon showers, amidst the horns and honks blaring from the Bombay traffic.

"Okay," he said, as if he was expecting the worst.

"Arjun, I've been doing a lot of thinking and it's become clear to me that I'm just not ready for marriage ... I'm really sorry ..." I said, my voice trembling almost as much as my knees.

"What? Where's this coming from? Have I done something to upset you? Tell me honestly. You know you can tell me anything."

"No, no. It's not you. You're the kindest, sweetest, most amazing guy I know. You're way better than I deserve." My guilt jumped to the surface. "It's not you, Arjun, it's me. I've realised that I have so much to learn, so many things I need to work out in my own self. Until I do, I just won't make a good partner for you with all my issues."

"But why are you saying all this? You're fantastic. I adore you. I don't want to be with anyone else. There's nothing wrong with you. Are you maybe just scared?" He sounded bewildered.

"No, no. I mean, it's true that I'm scared, but because I know I have so much more to learn and discover. I'm just not ready for you," I tried to explain, but felt I was doing a bad job.

"But I don't understand. I thought you loved me? I thought you wanted to be with me, too?"

"I do, I still do."

"Then what's the problem?" he snapped. "We'll figure things out along the way. We'll take it step by step ..."

The more he tried to persuade me, the clearer I became about what I felt and had to do. My mind and body calmed down there and then. I knew now for certain, with my whole being, that loving him as much as I did—hurt him as I would—I couldn't get married so young. I first had to establish myself in life.

"It's really not you, Arjun. I'm so, so, so sorry for hurting you. I hope that one day you'll forgive me. All I know, with all my heart, is that I have so much to learn and do before I can be worthy of someone like you," I said.

He went silent, as what I said sank in. "I don't know what else to say or do to change your mind." Then, in a small, broken voice, he asked "Is there someone else?

Don't you love me anymore?" He sounded tearful, barely able to say the words.

"Of course, I love you. A part of me always will." I wished I could put my arms around him and comfort him.

"You're everything to me. How can you do this? I cannot imagine being without you," he said as I heard thunder once more in Bombay, followed by another deluge of the monsoon. A gush of wind splashed a bucketload of rain against the glass panes of the red London phone box. It was dark, wet, miserable and dreary the whole world over, it seemed.

"And I can't imagine my life without you, either," I wept with regret. "I know it sounds like a worn-out cliche, but it's the truth—in my life, you really are the best thing that's ever happened to me. I might now be making the stupidest mistake of my entire life but no matter how I try, I just have to do what I know I have to do. I simply can't do justice to you. You're very special and you deserve the best. I have to discover something of myself before I can bring something truly valuable into a relationship."

Tears washed down my face while it still rained cats and dogs outside.

"Hello? Hello? Can you hear me? Are you still there?" Arjun's voice came through the continuous bleeps that warned me the money was about to run out. I scrambled to put yet more coins into the phone.

"I'm here."

"But I still don't understand. We're so good together. Everyone thinks we're perfect for each other. Everyone's going to be so upset. You're going to hurt a lot of people, besides me. Don't you care about that?"

I cried out loudly, almost wailing with despair. "I don't *want* to hurt anyone, least of all you."

"Well, you're doing a damn good job of it." He sounded so angry.

"Oh, please, don't take it that way. I really don't want to hurt you."

"That's too bad. You can't tell me how I have to feel."

"Oh, Arjun, please don't hate me. We've been such good friends for so long. Maybe, one day, we could be friends again?"

He remained quiet for a while, then said, "So this is the end, then?"

"Oh no, please don't let this be the end. I can't imagine not being close to you, not being friends," I said, unable to bear the finality of the thought.

"This is too painful," he said.

"I'm really sorry. I wish it could be different." I failed to find more apt words.

"As much as you hurt me, I only want the best for you. I hope you'll find what you're looking for," he said, finally accepting. "Maybe it's best if we don't talk to each other for a while."

My heart sank into despair, genuinely wishing I knew another way. "I'm really, really sorry. I can't say it enough. I'll miss you."

I hung up the phone.

Exhausted and drained, I leaned onto the side of the phone box with that sinking feeling. What would I do without that wonderful guy in my life? It was as if I had just amputated a precious part of me. This was the toughest conversation of my life. Even tougher than plucking up the courage to tell my dad that I was not ready to get married. Yet, I felt deeply sad and relieved for having been honest in telling Arjun how I felt. No sooner had I stepped out of the phone box, the downpour of rain ceased.

That evening, I came home from work, prepared to tell my dad that I had spoken to Arjun and told him everything. As it turned out, Papa had already been home and gone out again, but my mum told me that Arjun's mother, naturally concerned, had called shortly after my call to Arjun. Mum said that Arjun hadn't told his mother the details of our conversation, but she gathered from how upset he was that it must have been something significant. Papa discussed it with Arjun's mother later and had now gone to meet with Grandad Bapuji to talk it over with him, too.

With Papa shielding me, I never did find out what was said between him and my grandad, nor with anyone else. I felt wholly responsible for casting distress and sadness on our families and I vowed to myself that, in the fullness of time, something golden had to emerge from it.

"Simple it may sound,
easy it is not: developing
unwavering trust in your
own power and ability to create
and direct your life is the biggest
gift you can give yourself."

# 14

## Bold Beginnings

This one event springboarded me fast out of my teens and into adulthood. It sharpened my focus, igniting a fire in my belly for *making* my life and not merely being at the *mercy* of it.

I carried on living with my parents over the next five or six months after my conversation with Arjun. The store that I managed had been doing very well but I craved to do more. When I was told that it would have to be closed for a month for refurbishment, I grabbed the opportunity to take that time off and search for pastures new.

I yearned to have my own place but that just did not seem possible. Two problems in particular seemed insurmountable. The first was that I didn't have nearly enough money saved of my own. The second hurdle was bigger and it appeared impassable, especially so soon after I had only just caused what felt, to our families, like a cultural catastrophe from which they would need years to recover. The hurdle? In my culture, it was a taboo: women simply did not live alone.

Then, there was the matter of healing the traumas and scars from my childhood from when my mum had been so horribly ill. I realised now that, while being cocooned living in the hubbub of my big extended family, I had managed to suppress feeling the turmoil that lay beneath. Those wounds remained, festering just under the surface. They had a life of their own, and would erupt unexpectedly as bouts of sadness or anger. Being around my parents day in and day out, I could not figure out how to untangle myself from them energetically and psychologically. So much confusion filled my head. Which aspect of what I felt, thought, and knew myself to be, was really me? How much of it came from things I had simply 'picked up' from them or been conditioned with from the family? To be whole, it was important to work out these questions and, selfish or not, I gasped for space in which I could do that.

During the month off work, while my store was undergoing the refit, I looked in the national newspaper adverts for jobs that would appeal to me. I had turned twenty-one three months ago and, while running a store had taught me a great deal about generating revenues, training staff for excellent sales and customer service, merchandising seasonal fashion, and so on, I was capable of much, much more. I fancied myself being out and about, working with senior executives of large companies, generating business from the topmost floors in the well-known institutions of the city of London. I could see myself earning way more than I was doing right now and I had to find a way of doing it.

Within days of starting my search, I met with a recruitment agent who was thrilled to have me on his books. He sent me off to be interviewed for a sales role with one of the top telecoms companies across the UK and America. One psychometric profiling test and three interviews later, each one more rigorous than the last, I was offered the job within just two weeks. It came with the promise of industry-renowned business development training, a car, a basic salary, a high-earning bonus potential, and I would be working in central London.

This was just fantastic and more than I could have hoped for. The training turned out to be excellent. Even more than giving me a good foundation of essential business, sales, and negotiation skills, it unleashed a hidden talent for doing business that I had no idea I possessed. In the years to come, winning business with innovative services, or in new domains, or establishing long-term relationships with customers where others had failed, became my forte.

From the very first day, even though I was the only woman in a large team, I loved my job. It suited me perfectly. I had freedom to go about doing my work as I pleased, so long as I produced the results, and this challenge set me ablaze. It tended the fire in my belly that had ignited some months before. Within the first three months of starting the job, I raced ahead of the targets set and though I worked hard, it did not feel like 'hard work'. After a while, doing what I loved to do, it felt more like play than 'work'. Within eight months of starting this job, I had earned enough money to put down a deposit for a two-bedroom apartment in Greater London, with enough saved for furnishing and decorating it. I also qualified for a series of incentives for higher achievers, including lunches at top London restaurants and trips abroad. This was way more than even I could have dreamt up. Now I could, after all, have a place of my own. I could buy it and my parents would understand that rather than leaving them, I was making an investment. That was not at all the same thing as renting, just to get away from them. This was more acceptable, surely?

I hoped and prayed that they would understand. I knew well that, even then, it would not be easy for them. In England, even in the latter part of the twentieth century, there were hardly any precedents of Indian girls, and guys for that matter, leaving the family home and having their own place. If they needed to stay away during the week for work, they were surely expected to return home most weekends. Independence was seen as a threat. Being called *azaadi* (freedom-loving) was a term used disparagingly in my culture. It contained a whole litany of meaning that was denigrating.

In spite of this, my soul longed for space and time to figure out what life was all about.

Desperately, I hoped that my parents would understand the reason I sought to buy my own place. It wasn't because I intended to stay out all hours of the night and drink myself into oblivion, or that I had in mind to gallivant all over the place, seeking empty pleasures. I hoped my family would understand me and know my character better than that.

House hunting was awkward, not having told my family that I was doing this. It wasn't normal but expected that big decisions were not made on your own, single-handedly. They had to be discussed and agreed with the parents and elders of the family. Whatever I did, it would only bring up a fearful response, and they would never in a million years agree. What was I to do?

As the date for completion on the purchase of my apartment came closer, I finally plucked up the courage to tell my dad. "Papa, I have some wonderful news," I announced one evening. "I've found a two-bedroom flat that I want to buy. We'll be completing the signing of the contact in a few days." I expected Papa to explode with anger. Instead, his face broke out in the biggest surprised smile.

"That's amazing news!" he exclaimed. "I had no idea. Why didn't you tell me about this before, that you wanted to buy a property?" My mum, in the meantime, hearing the excitement, had come into the living room. She, too, looked thrilled and grinned from ear to ear. She often talked about how, as a law student, she had spent many happy years away from home. She, however, had not lived completely alone but inside a community of college girls, so within the acceptable bounds of Indian society.

"Papa," I ventured, "I didn't tell you because I wasn't sure if you would allow me to buy it. You see, I've bought it so I can live in it." His face changed. He still looked proud as a pheasant, but suddenly, as I had anticipated, fear etched his face.

"Oh. I see," he said. I tried to explain to him why it was important for me to do this but he was lost in his own thoughts. "Why do you want to live separate from us? Aren't you happy here?" He looked upset.

"Of course I'm happy here, Papa," I said. "It's just that I want to experience more of life. I want to discover who I am, and what I can achieve on my own. I want to travel the world and learn so many things—"

Papa interrupted me. "But you can do all that from here. No one is stopping you."

"That's true. It's just that I feel I need to do this on my own, in my own way. I need to show myself, and you, that I can take responsibility for my life, that it's possible to succeed on my own terms." Even though I said all the right things, I could tell that as far as Papa was concerned, I might as well have been talking Martian.

"What's all this? Taking responsibility ... succeeding on your own terms ... I've never heard such gibberish!"

"But I want to make you proud."

"What more is there to be proud of? I'm already proud," he said.

"No, I mean, I want to make you proud, to support you—"

"You're our daughter. We don't have any right to expect you to support us. All I want is for you to get married, have children and be happy. That's all the reward we need." He wore a baffled expression. I was shocked to hear my dad say this. Was that all he wanted for me? "Then you can work or have a career all you like."

"That's just it, Papa. You don't see how much potential I have. I can do so much. I don't just want to get married and have children, not right now anyhow, and certainly not before I've had a chance to see what I can accomplish on my own. How can you say these things? If I was a boy, your aspirations for me wouldn't be so low, would they? I'm so disappointed, Papa, that that's all you want for me!"

"Look, I'm a broad-minded man but you can't just leave home and set up on your own. We just don't do things like that, especially being a girl. That's all fine for the Westerners."

"But Papa, why is it different for a girl? If I was your son, would you still object?" This distinction of sexes had always troubled me. "Who says I can't do just as well as, if not even better than, any guy?" I asked. "I simply don't accept that it has to be different for me because I'm a girl."

"If you were my son, I would still say the same thing," Papa said.

"No, you wouldn't, Papa. I'm sure of it. You would shout from the rooftops that your son had bought his first property with his own earnings at just twenty-one years of age." It was hopeless, being an Indian girl, even in the late twentieth century.

"Are you so unhappy living here, that you have to leave us and live somewhere on your own?" Papa asked me again, looking hurt.

"No, Papa, of course not. What reason would I have to be unhappy? And I'm not *leaving* you. You are wonderful parents, you and Mum. I know it must be difficult to understand, but it's really, really not like that."

I looked at him, pushing back tears of love that welled up behind my eyes. I wished he wouldn't look so hurt. I felt so responsible for his happiness. "It's just that I'd like to explore the world, learn more about who I am, and I can't do that when my every need is looked after by you. I want to understand the way the world works. I don't want to be a burden to you all my life, or to someone else. It's important to me that I can stand on my own feet. Soon, I will be able to support you, too." My heart went out to him and my mum. I went over and threw my arms around him. Why was life such a paradox? To find myself, why did I have to disappoint the very people I loved? There had to be an easier way, surely?

"I don't know where you're getting all these ideas from. We're Indians. We have never done things in that way," he said, still baffled. "How do you expect me to explain this to the others? Will they understand? I don't think so!" He gripped the arm of the chair, and gave a loud sigh. "How will I explain this to the family? Or to people in the community? It's just not the done thing, Meeta." Yet again, I had somehow managed to lumber my poor Papa with another socially unacceptable dilemma to deal with.

"Papa, why do you worry so much about what everyone else thinks? Where's the freedom in that? I can't live like that—worrying every step of the way about what everyone else will think. It's like being tied and boxed up. It makes me feel claustrophobic, and it's just a way to keep you living a safe, small life." I wanted to scream with the frustration that this brought up in me but instead, I held myself together, my chest tightening at the thought.

That was the truth of it for me and to my surprise and relief, Papa eventually understood. "Papa, don't you sometimes crave to be free, too?" I asked the question that I had often wondered. "If you were being really honest with me, wouldn't you say that you too wish you could discover a different side of the world to the one that you've always lived in?" His face softened and he nodded, even if only for a split second.

I knew then that I was merely a bolder reflection of my father's unfulfilled aspirations.

"That's all very well, *beta*, but we are not islands. We have to live within the *samaj*," he said.

*Samaj*, a Sanskrit word for society, was a word I had heard again and again in conversations. "What will *samaj* say?" "You have to do what's acceptable to *samaj*." "*Samaj* will discard you if you do that." It seemed to me that we were utterly dominated by the fear of what was acceptable to this faceless, anonymous so-called *samaj* and yet, who exactly was it that we were trying to please, sacrificing or rejecting even our soul's call for its faceless acceptance? And where was this so-called '*samaj*' when my mother was so horribly sick? Was it behind closed doors? It probably feasted on juicy gossip behind those doors. I felt somewhat acerbic.

"Papa, as long as you and Mum and Motima and Bapuji and Motabhai still love me, it doesn't much matter what others think. I promise you and Mum that I will not disappoint you." I hugged him again and then my mum. "And it's not like I'm leaving London. I'll still be around to speak to you on the phone every day and I'll be over to cause just as much mayhem as I always have done," I said, tearful, trying to inject some lightness.

"When did you grow up so much?" he said, finally smiling a little and tightening his arms around me.

Once again, I wished things could have been different. I wished that my path did not have to give my family so much consternation or force them into the discomfort of expanding their cultural boundaries. For years, I'd carried enormous guilt for putting them through these challenges, wishing I had been put together differently, in a way where I 'fitted in' with Indian traditions.

What I could not have known then, was that years later, I and others like me taking these bold and audacious steps, paved the way for the younger generations to have an easier time of enjoying such freedoms for themselves. In the twenty-first century, it would slowly become somewhat more acceptable in the British Indian culture, though still not completely, to integrate the Eastern and Western value systems. For me, however, claiming this freedom felt more traumatic than trailblazing. It certainly didn't seem like I was doing anything socially pioneering, which—in retrospect—is exactly what I had done.

"If there is such a thing as
being a master of your destiny,
it needs you to become conscious
of which stresses and traumas
are still looping within you,
however much in the background
they might be."

# 15

## Abrupt Endings

Five months flew by.

I settled into my new apartment, and completed one full year in my job.

I had settled into a routine in my new home and after the difficult choices of the last months, life was now finally much lighter. At work, I soared with effortless ease, breaking one target after another, earning one incentive bigger than the last. I really liked the people I worked with. We all got on well with each other and helped out when one of us needed a last minute push to meet our targets. Everything was going swimmingly well.

Then, as usual for a Monday morning, I went to work. This morning, however, I was called in to see the managing director. He sat me down and told me that business had not been as good as expected for the company, and he had to scale down the sales team by letting go of several people. This, he said, meant that he was having to make me redundant. I could not believe what I was hearing, and argued that I had consistently been the salesperson of the month and could not understand why I was being selected for redundancy. He said that firing anybody was hard and so he was firing the newest and youngest, and my fourteen glorious months came to an abrupt end.

Later that morning, after packing my things, I went back home by train, having been obliged to give back my company car. I was in total shock, and up a creek with no paddle. How could things have changed so suddenly, from being at the top of my game to being down and out? This, in my world, felt like rejection. Was there something wrong with me? Did the director just fob me off with a nonsense explanation, saying he was letting go of the newest and youngest? My career had just started and I could not fathom a future. I could not see how I would be able to explain this to a potential employer. Would they believe me? Having lost my fantastic job, I felt stupid and ashamed. Somehow, I had failed.

Obviously, I wasn't good enough.

With all my savings spent on buying and furnishing my flat, I had only enough to live on for less than a month. I was on the brink of losing everything, but there was no way that I could turn back to my family. I dared not face the bank manager. After all, he had only just given me my mortgage. With no means to repay them, I couldn't dream of borrowing from my friends, either.

"What on earth am I going to do now?" I said to myself that evening, hemmed into my flat. I was in the grip of sheer terror about my future. Was this what it meant to be free and independent? There was absolutely no one I could turn to for help, least of all my parents, for whom this would just be another source of worry that they did not need.

With no car and soon no flat either, I was sick with worry. Having made such a big splash at home once again, this time to move out, what was I going to tell my family? The last thing I wanted was to admit defeat, and in less than six months from leaving home, too.

In despair and panicking for a few hours, I couldn't see my way forward. I had to get out of my flat and clear my head. A stunned zombie, that evening I went out for a walk in our local park. I walked up and down the park and round and round and round and round its cycling path, oblivious to my surroundings.

What am I going to do now? What am I going to do now? What am I going to do now?

Eventually, as the daylight gave in to dusk, I sat down on one of the park benches. My head was swirling with terror—terror of having no money, terror of what I would tell my family, terror of how I would ever get another job. Who would want to employ me, now that I'd had this monumental fall from grace? Compared to the agony and fear I felt now, truly all alone, standing up to my family to decline getting married and telling them I was moving out was child's play, like baby lion cubs sparring. *This* was the real stuff of life. I wanted to learn about life and what it was all about. I was just beginning to realise that this was it. This is what real life was all about.

Drained and heavy with worry, unable to get myself up, I passed out there and then on a park bench in the pitch black of the night. The park warden must have been on his evening off that day because I found myself awakened the next morning by rays of dawn, flickering and dancing like sparkling diamonds through spaces between the leaves of the trees and bushes. In my semi-conscious, dreamlike state, I heard a soft voice say, *"It's time to wake up!"* It was the call of my Inner Diamond. In that half-awake, half-asleep state, I dropped into a deep dialogue with it.

"I'm terrified and ashamed of myself! I thought I was doing really well. How can I ever face anyone again? No one will hire me ever again. And I'm still at the start of my working life. I'll have to go back home, with my tail between my legs. I never want to wake up again. I can't face the world."

Softly, the Inner Diamond replied, *'The lesson here is to never take anything for granted, because there are no certainties in life."*

"I don't understand," I said, sinking into the depths of fear.

*"First of all, remember when you were seven and you were upset? Do you remember what you were told then?"*

I thought for a moment. "Yes, I remember hearing that I will always be taken care of."

*"That's right. You are taken care of. Know that always."*

Simply remembering this, helped to ease a little of the fear that gripped me.

*"Fear of the unknown paralyses people. Become a master of flowing with uncertainty,"* the Diamond replied.

"But everybody will think I was fired. They will probably think I was bad at my job. How will I explain this away to another potential employer?" I asked in desperation.

*"Remember that conversation at the riverside about learning to trust yourself. Simple it may sound, easy it is not:*

developing unwavering trust in your own power and ability to create and direct your life is the biggest gift you can give yourself. Standing in absolute self-conviction, let them see what great service you can be to them."

"How can I trust myself when my emotions are up and then down and up again. They're like massive waves that throw me about from one unstable place to another. I have no control over how I feel because things just happen to me. How can I trust myself?" I asked, agitated.

"It's all about your perspective, how you see things," came its reply. "Especially, how you see yourself. You see, others mirror back to you what you are projecting of yourself onto them. Being ashamed for not feeling good enough, you are merely projecting your insecurity and then you sell yourself short. That's not who you are. Remember! You are a brilliant, vibrant spark of the Divine!"

"Can you please tell me, how can I feel that, this sense of being a vibrant spark, especially when I have no control over how awful I feel?" I asked.

"You see, your emotions are the waves at the surface of the sea, where it's nothing but turbulence. So, in those moments when you feel you have no control, learn to dive away from the surface and deeper into the ocean that is your mind. No matter *how choppy things are at the surface, below you will find it calmer, clear and still."*

I listened with all my senses, letting these teachings sink into my being. The park's lake, near the bench where I lay, glistened as the rays of the morning sun glinted off its still surface. The Inner Diamond continued.

*"You can recognise your deeper Self through these essential qualities. Once there, in the domain of clarity, you will be able to take hold of the reins of your thoughts, choosing those that serve you, and not being at the mercy of the ones that harm you."*

"Are you saying that I'm strong enough to overcome anything, if only I were able to trust myself to do it?" I asked, aware of how my insecurities influenced my every thought.

*"Yes. Everyone is."*

"When I'm so upset, I can't see the wood for the trees. I get caught up in the intensity of what I'm feeling and I almost completely forget who I am," I said.

*"Start by reminding yourself of those good things you have accomplished already and, especially, the qualities that you have that made this possible. Discipline your mind to*

*frequently spot random or unhelpful thoughts and direct it to seek the highest outcomes, instead of resisting your inner power, because it is always energising you, whether you know it or not. Simply by bringing your awareness to its presence, you can open to it. Let it stream into your thoughts and let only such empowered thoughts guide your action."* This uplifting guidance snapped my thoughts out of my drama and into purposeful action.

Every time I had encountered my Inner Diamond, it had transmitted a special energy that had me find the courage lurking deep within me. It had, once again, through just a few wise words, set me on course. With renewed confidence and inspiration, I bounced up from the park bench, went home, and showered. When I looked in the mirror, I saw not the girl who had just lost her job, but a woman with a vision to fulfil. That day, I even did my hair and make-up differently to how I'd always done it.

Intrepid, I took the bus to the bank that morning to meet my bank manager. He sensed my confidence and self-assuredness, and granted me a new loan that would help me through the next few months while I found another job. I called all the recruitment agents that I had met some months before and set about looking for another opportunity in which I could grow and thrive.

As my Inner Diamond had declared, this was its call for me to 'wake up'. It was time to begin discovering and becoming, layer upon layer, a conscious expression of the essence of who I really was.

"You must learn to take responsibility
for the way you are designed
so that you can
be free to be yourself."

# 16

# Cardboard Cut-out

After losing my last job, in the months to come I was offered jobs in business development with technology companies. I worked temporarily with an organisation for six months while I looked for something more permanent. It wasn't too long before I found a role with a company that was just perfect for me. A small team of young entrepreneurs ran it and my go-getter spirit fitted right in. My job was to take their then state of the art, innovative call centre technology to the senior management of mid-sized to large corporations and have them modernise the way they handled telephone calls. One day, I could be driving to the centre of London talking to the management of a well-known bank or insurance company, the next day to meet with a large telecoms service provider in Birmingham, and the day after going to see the manufacturer of medical products in Hull. For someone in her early twenties, the whole prospect of having responsibility for developing business with such a diverse clientele, changing the way that these companies addressed their customers and helping to build a business from scratch was as exciting as it was absorbing.

Over the next three years, I relished surpassing the targets set in my work, which I did regularly, learning new skills and tapping into ones that I didn't know I had. Discovering how the world of business worked was fascinating. It felt second nature to me, and conquering new business challenges was nothing short of exhilarating. It was easy to settle into a day-to-day routine and heave a big sigh of relief to have my money problems well and truly behind me, especially without my family's intervention. I went from strength to strength at work and earned well.

On a personal emotional front, however, a contrast had emerged. The more settled and successful I became in my work, the less secure or happy I felt. The turmoil of trauma from my past that lurked within me, beneath the surface, had whirled into my awareness and cast its dark, gloomy shadow in my emotional landscape.

The feeling that something substantial, as well as someone, was missing, bubbled up within but had not yet become obvious to me. And so, I went about my business as usual. That is, until a conversation with my good friend Gina.

"Gina! How have you been, girl? I'm so happy to see you! I've missed you," I cried on seeing her emerge from the Saturday afternoon London crowds. After a long hug, with a broad smile, she examined my face.

I hadn't seen Gina since she had left to go and work in New York, the Christmas just after I had bought my flat.

The Covent Garden Piazza, where we were sitting, buzzed with locals and tourists alike, enjoying the sunshine and taking in the acts being performed by the mime artists nearby. Covent Garden was one of my favourite places in London and whenever I got together with friends, I would suggest meeting there. It had an unusual appeal. Modern shops and restaurants blended into the charm of a bygone London that dated as far back as the first century, when a Roman settlement sprung up here, calling it Londonium. The Saxons, in the seventh century, made the Covent Garden area into a thriving trading port call Lundenwic, which became considered too dangerous and consequently abandoned in the ninth century with the invasion of the Vikings. I felt unusually connected to this place, where the Romans, Saxons and Vikings had walked through and now, and where Gina and I were soaking up its rich atmosphere.

It was the very first weekend of Gina's return to London and I was so happy to see her.

"You left so suddenly when you took off for New York. I've really missed you," I said, still feeling the delight of being with Gina after three years that felt like at least five. She had been one of my closest friends before she had left and had been perhaps my only support during the difficult time when I had made my choice not to get married.

Gina and I met when I was a teenager, working on Saturdays and holidays in a London store to earn some money while I was studying. Gina was at least fifteen years older than me and she, as a student herself, worked part-time at the same store for a couple of years, before finding the right role in her chosen career. Regardless of our age difference, we got on very well and continued to be friends, despite moving on to do different things in our work. As a child, Gina had spent several summers and other holidays in India with her Italian mother, who had been a hippy—a spiritual seeker learning yoga, meditation and Indian philosophies. This gave Gina a view into my world, and common ground where we could connect.

"I know. It's been one hell of a journey in the last three years," she replied.

"I never quite understood why you had to leave so suddenly? You were here one week and just disappeared the next?" I asked. Since Gina left for New York, we had barely had the chance to speak at all.

"Well, my predecessor in New York had to leave quite suddenly and there was a high profile programme that needed to be continued without gaps. So my company offered me his position, with the caveat of starting more or less immediately. My divorce had just come through that same week. I'd been thinking about a fresh start somewhere else and it seemed almost too good an opportunity to miss."

A waiter approached our table and interrupted us. "What can I get you beautiful ladies on this fine evening?" he said, in a charming Italian accent.

We ordered a bottle of Chablis to complement the hot summer's evening and asked for more time to place the order for our meal.

"Was it a promotion?" I asked.

"Yep! Something I didn't think was possible from inside my company," she beamed.

"What's your role?"

"Senior Vice President of Human Resources, which included the talent development, leadership training, and so on," Gina said.

I teased, "Senior! Yep! That's you! You are, after all, getting old and wrinkly."

"Oi! Less of the old and wrinkly and more of the young and wise!" Gina grinned.

"Haha! You know I'm just jesting. You look amazing, for your age," I couldn't help pulling her leg. "Seriously, though, how amazing that you got the promotion you really wanted. I'm so happy for you. Did the job live up to its expectations? Was New York really as fast and furious as it's made out to be?" I was curious.

"You bet," Gina said. "It's a whole other world when it comes to dealing with people. And I used my spare time to do an MSc in Human Behaviour and Design that I'd wanted to do for a long time."

"Wow! That's fantastic. So your colleagues had better watch out even more—you're even more of a lethal weapon than before." Although I teased, I couldn't help admiring Gina. She inspired me. "Did you meet anyone special there? And what village was he from? What is father's good name?" I put on my Gujarati Indian accent.

"Actually, I did. It was just the perfect relationship for a few years. We had a wonderful time going to shows on Broadway, fantastic restaurants. We took a few weekend trips to other parts of America. And just before it was time for me to come back to London, the relationship had run its natural course and we brought it to an end. Now that I think about it, the timing couldn't have been more impeccable," Gina said, with a somewhat wistful look.

"Did it help you to put the past behind you with your ex-husband, being in a new environment, a new challenge and the romance?" I asked.

"You know, I couldn't have asked for more. It was exactly what the doctor ordered. It would've taken perhaps a bit longer here." Gina nodded.

"Well, I can't wait to see what's next for you," I said.

Our waiter, now just a little edgy with impatience, was back. "Bella, Bella! I don't want you to pass out with starvation. Can I get you something to eat?"

Though deep in conversation, we felt obliged to be seen to be making the effort to look through the extensive menu. We sent the waiter away with an order of starters. We asked for more time again to decide on our main course. The waiter all but rolled his glossy chestnut eyes in despair.

Just as he walked away, as if out of the blue a blond man who looked like he was in his early thirties, walked over to our table. "I hope you won't mind me interrupting you. My name is Sean. I've been admiring you since you walked in. I think you're absolutely gorgeous." He held out his hand to shake mine. I was taken aback since I hadn't noticed him at all. "Thank you. It's very kind of you to take the trouble to say so. This is my friend, Gina." I said, indicating her. She had that mischievous expression on her face, obviously tickled at the guy's cheeky approach.

"May I call you sometime?" he asked, oozing charm and confidence. He had the manner of someone who was used to success. I wondered if he worked in the City as a trader or an investment banker.

"Call me? Why would you want to do that?" I said coolly, equally self-assured. I had no interest in forwarding this encounter.

He rose to the challenge. "Because I'd love to get to know you. I think there's something very special about you."

"Haha!" I laughed. "I bet you say that to all the girls."

"Actually, I know you may not believe me, but it's really not my style to approach women in this way," he said, looking apologetic.

I didn't buy any of it. "Haha! You're right. I don't believe you."

"Well, look, here's my business card. I'd love to meet up for a drink. Please, think about it and if you change your mind, give me a call," he said, ever so humbly and sweetly, and then left the restaurant with his friend who had been waiting for him at their table.

Gina looked like she needed the serviette to wipe her laughing eyes. "Ohhhh! He was gorgeous. And how sweet was that!"

She grabbed his business card from my hand. "Oooh, he's one of those traders for one of the large banks in Europe, too. You should definitely give him a call." Gina was being tongue in cheek but meant it too.

"Yeah! Yeah! What's the big deal? None of them can be trusted when push comes to shove," I said dismissively, a bit bitter with cynicism.

"What? He was lovely. And I think he really meant what he said."

"Yeah, maybe," I said, still unmoved.

"What's the matter with you, girl? You didn't see him looking at you, did you? I noticed him staring at you through the window as soon as we sat down. See now, you didn't used to miss a trick."

"Oh! What's the big deal? I'm fine." I waved my hand in a dismissive gesture.

Gina laid into me. "No, that's not like you at all. Normally you're much more open, funny, feisty. You were nonchalant with the waiter too, even though he's a charming, romantic guy. That's two men in the space of a few minutes that both melted my heart while they needed an ice pick to hack open yours. That's just not like you. That's not the same Smita I used to go out with at all. What's going on with you, sweetie?" She paused to give me a long stare.

"Come to think of it, you do look lovely as usual, but there's something subtly different about you," she said. "That sparkle of yours is missing. You're here but you're not your bubbly, vibrant self. It's like a part of you is here but the rest of you has gone AWOL. What's going on with you?"

"Really? Can you tell all that?" I replied, putting on my bravest face. "Everything's going great guns at work. I love my job and there's no one to make demands on me. No one to control me. Life couldn't be better." I grinned to try and hide the cyclone that whirled around in my inner world, making me feel heavy and unsettled.

The culture I had grown up in was not one where you put your real feelings on display, unless they were ones of jubilation. To show your deeper feelings wasn't just frowned upon, it was treated with disdain. It was considered not only imprudent but positively foolish, as it would make you prey to gossip. No, no, no: showing your true feelings was indulgent and betrayed a weak character. No, strong, at all times. This is what you needed to be. Besides, showing your real feelings made you vulnerable and the person you shared them with uncomfortable. In our culture, vulnerability equalled weakness. So it wasn't an option but a concrete necessity to barricade your real feelings with the strongest bricks and stones from others, unless they were feelings that made you look good.

On the other hand, I was an abject failure at this game of camouflage. Try as I might to hide my feelings, I could not do it to save my life. Even my conditioning from my childhood days of needing to be a 'good girl' didn't work when I really needed it to.

"Something's definitely different about you," Gina persisted, like a dog with a bone. "You're suffering in silence about something. So are you going to tell me what's going on or am I going to have to prise it out of you?"

Gina was one of the few people who had been able to understand me completely and now that she had got an MSc in Human Behaviour and Design, there was no escaping her.

Annoyed with myself for being so utterly transparent but, at the same time, realising that I needed help, I made a reluctant attempt to dig within. "I don't really know where to begin. I've got a whirlwind of feelings going on. I don't even know which one to start with," I said, hot with shame as I caught my inner critic chiding me: I should have done a better job of sorting myself out already!

"So start from anywhere, it doesn't matter. Talk about what's right there for you, don't worry about putting it in order."

I had forgotten what it was like to be genuinely cared for. "Well, I now have everything as I wanted it and yet I feel like there's a gaping hole in my life." I took a sip of the Chablis to relieve the dryness in my mouth.

The culture in which I grew up concealed personal imperfection with secret shame and my inner critic had sprung into overdrive, admonishing me for my failure to be perfect.

"I've been waking up with dread in the pit of my stomach, as if dark, stormy clouds are whirling around inside me." I shuffled in my seat, as uncomfortable in this conversation as sitting on a searing stove on a sweltering summer's day.

As I got in touch with my emotional chaos, I felt my legs drain of energy. It dawned on me just how much power it had over me, leaving me feeling helpless, even hopeless.

How imprisoned was I? I fixated on how I came across even to Gina, who was my good friend. Would Gina ever think of me the same way again? This was the legacy of my cultural upbringing, the unconscious drive to be perfect and feeling secret shame when you were not, secret because even feeling shame was a mark of a flawed character. "You should not feel ashamed about anything," I could hear the Indian accent of my mother ringing in my ears. I would later come to realise that the Indian culture of 'shoulds' and 'should nots' had long had me tied me up in knots.

I should have been able to sort this out myself. I'm obviously not as clever as I thought I was. The megaphone of my inner critic resounded with such thoughts, except I was entirely clueless.

Gina said, "Tell me about what it is that you're feeling. See if you can put words to that feeling of dread in your stomach and those dark, heavy clouds. If they were emotions and feelings, what would they be? What are you actually feeling?"

This was typical Gina, probing and trying to unravel my unarticulated, emotional whirlwind.

I tried to explain but felt gripped in my throat. I didn't even know how to put words to my turmoil. I felt numb. All I could come up with were clues through what I did because I couldn't reach into what I felt. "When I'm not at work, I hardly go out, except to buy the groceries and, at weekends, I avoid going out altogether. Some weekends, I go to bed on a Friday night and wake up over the weekend only to shower and maybe, if I'm really starving, I'll eat something. The rest of the time, I stay in bed and sleep."

Until now this had been my guilty secret but, in sharing it with another person, it had somehow become more real. "I'm a hermit at weekends."

Gina listened intently. "Oh sweetie, why haven't you said anything before?" she asked, concerned. "I had no idea. Well, look, I'm back to London now, I'm here—"

I interrupted her in mid-sentence as my numbness was starting to wear off. "Before even getting started, I walk away from possibilities of romantic relationships with men who dare to like me. But then, time and again, I find myself being attracted to men who are charismatic and charming but turn out to be totally unavailable or just complete jerks. I find out they're spoken for, often pretending not to be. So I run as far as I can from them and push away the ones who might be worth considering. In any case, they're all non-starters and I continue to be alone." My voice quivered as my deeper fears surfaced, afraid that they might be real.

Just then, to inject irony to my situation and as if the gods were listening in on our conversation and wanting a good laugh, yet another man—this time an older chap—approached our table with a bunch of single red roses in his hand. He was giving them away in return for a donation to charity of a pound or two. I shook my head at him, willing him to go away. After all, I hadn't yet plummeted to the desperate depths that would have me buy myself a single red rose.

"Do you think I'll ever fall in love again, Gina? Why don't I feel passion for life like I used to? Am I not able to commit? Like you said earlier, what is wrong with me? It's like I'm stuck in some one-way maze that I can't find my way out of."

Then, as if there really was some cosmic joke being played out, a rather large woman, whose hair would have greatly benefitted from a much-needed shampoo, walked towards us as she crossed the Piazza. She wore a bright yellow T-shirt with red letters that ran across her well-endowed chest. The red letters said, "Please don't fall in love with me!" Really? You couldn't make it up if you tried.

Gina and I looked at each other and, though I was in the midst of getting in touch with the pain of my trauma, we fell about laughing hysterically at the stupendous irony of this drama. I cried out, "There you go! I'm so unconscious that I need a complete stranger to brazenly flaunt the words I must obviously have tattooed across my forehead!"

The fears that had been trickling into my conscious awareness in the dead hours of night, awakening me with dread in the pit of my stomach, now erupted in full flow, casting a smudged shadow over my view of who I thought I was. Where was this coming from? "To make matters worse, I've hardly been to see my parents of late, and even less other members of my family. I hardly see even my friends these days."

Gina absorbed what I said and, more importantly, what I was unable to say. "There's nothing wrong with you. You mustn't even entertain that thought," she said. "You're allowed to be just a little angry at a culture and people that tried to bully you into doing things their way. And that's bound to have tested your trust in men, don't you think? Just give it time, sweetie. I know you. You're not someone who's designed to go through life bitter and dysfunctional. You're a warrior. You'll find ways of healing all these wounds and come away soaring."

Somehow, she had catalysed the process of unlocking my emotional floodgates and now that I had started, I couldn't stop. "Maybe. Right now, I just feel utter sadness, not so much anger. And until I just said what I said, I hadn't got a clue that I'd stopped trusting men."

"Sure. But remember that sadness and anger are two sides of the same coin. The important thing is to allow what's there to come to the surface, notice it's there, embrace it by accepting it's there and then give it permission to leave. Which one comes up first is not important. What matters is that they don't stay stuck, denied and unacknowledged in you for too long, because that's when they can do damage," Gina said.

I nodded, hanging on to her every word, somewhat despairingly. "It used to be that I felt so connected to my higher Self, what I call my 'Inner Diamond'. Or so I thought. But now, I can just vaguely remember it. I can't hear or feel it." In the midst of starting to get present to the sticky conundrum that was my life, I looked at Gina, panicked by the intensity of the emerging deluge of sadness, hidden anger, self-doubt and hopelessness.

"Was the Inner Diamond just a figment of my imagination, Gina? Did I make it all up? Have I become so numb, so unconscious, that I can barely feel what's going on within me? It's as if my capacity to feel things is blunted. I shouldn't be feeling like this. Especially when things are finally going well for me." An acute pain intensified in my abdomen.

"It's still there. Remember when you decided not to get married, you had a compelling intuition that you had to wait and work on discovering your true inner Self." Gina reminded me.

"Huh huh," I nodded, still in the depths of despair.

"Well, all that's happened and what it's left you to deal with, are guideposts to the areas within you that you'll have to work on healing. Then you can know who you are beneath the clutter of emotions and suffering.

You'll discover the real you, beyond the illusion of who it seems you are," Gina said.

"Well, meanwhile, I feel like a cardboard cut-out of myself. Two-dimensional with no depth," I said, looking in at myself from the outside, like a fly on the wall.

Gina's soft face had kindness written all over it and she reached out to stroke the back of my hand. She was more in my world, she understood me more at this moment, than I understood myself. Or, indeed, had ever been understood. In doing so, she had given me the gift of activating my healing, and much, much more: the process of becoming self-aware.

"I've got just the perfect present for you from New York." Gina's attention got hijacked just as she reached into her handbag, when our charming Italian waiter came over once again and demanded that we place our order for the main course.

We stopped talking long enough to order and he disappeared back into the restaurant, which was now filled to capacity. We did the right thing to arrive early and make one of the open air tables our home for the evening. Though it was now almost nine o'clock, the cloudless sky was bright, and promising a beautiful sunset.

"It's about
accepting and owning our feelings,
no matter how painful,
rather than
avoiding or deleting them."

# 17

# Don't Fall In Love With Me

The bar-goers and nightclubbers filed past us thick and fast, filling up the Piazza. The women looked as if they had stepped off the cover of *Cosmopolitan* with remnants of the super trendy 1980's permed tresses, or hair crimped like lions' manes, or Princess Diana lookalikes with short, flicked-back styles, rara skirts and matching high heels, sandals and handbags. And men with slicked-back smooth hair in baggy carpenter trousers, and black leather jackets, or in spiky super-gelled hairstyles with acid wash denim jeans and Doc Marten boots, or chaps in neon-coloured trainers with flashing lights,and well-stacked flat tops or hi-top fade cuts that looked like bird's nests. They made interesting viewing in the Piazza.

"If it wasn't for my pathetic, messed up life in which I've become a sorry cardboard cut-out of a figure, we could be sitting here having a good bellyching laugh at just watching these trendy dudes and dudettes pass by!" I lamented.

"Oh, sweetie, you're anything but a cardboard cut-out. Like all of us, you just need to learn how to unlock your depth and power, learn who you are beneath the shallow surface that you think you are. Also, you've had a lot to contend with ever since you were just a little girl. Now that you've had time and space away from your childhood home, all those experiences that left a mark on you will come to the surface," Gina said.

"Oh no! Why? Wasn't it enough to have to go through them in the first place? Must you suffer all your life because of things that were outside your control?" I said, horrified at the thought. "Or because of standing for what you believe to be right for you?"

"Ah, but only those things that are still unresolved within you have any power over you and it's those things that you can now allow to surface, in the safety of your new life, so that you can let them go, float away," she said, reassuring me. "It's a question of becoming more self-aware, which allows healing. You've had to make some courageous choices in your life, by anybody's standards, and you're still so young. You had to mature at supersonic speed and face difficult realities that are disturbing even for grown adults. Your mum, for example. What was the worst thing for you about your mum's illness?"

"That I couldn't reach her. It seemed like no one could to get through. She looked tormented, like she was in another world, and I couldn't do anything about it. I felt so disconnected from her. It made me feel lonely, and very, very sad and powerless. It's as if I went into a black hole that I haven't been able to climb out of," I said, as the anaesthesia that had made me numb lifted some more. "The worst thing about it was that no one talked about it. It was the big white elephant in the room and when someone did venture into the subject, there was a heavy, resigned, gloom and doom about it." I stared into the empty space of Covent Garden's central Piazza, as if summoning up that white elephant. "Even after all these years, the pain of seeing her so unwell, of not being able to reach out to her, is just as raw now as it was then."

"Hmmm ... what happened then is still unresolved in you." Gina took a bite of her pizza.

"What do you mean, 'unresolved'?" I asked. I knew what the word meant, but was unsure how Gina meant it in relationship to me. I was clearly a novice at this self-awareness business.

"So, what I mean by 'unresolved' is that you can still feel it just as it if it happened yesterday and it still has a grip on you. Though the incident or event itself might have happened years ago, and you may not even think about it now, it could continue to control how you react. It's all the more deceptive because it's not something you often think about. You can even believe that because it's in the past, it's over. But it's not. It very much defines who you are in the now, how you feel, how you perceive things. It becomes the lens through which you perceive what happens in your life now," Gina said.

"See, when something happens that you find deeply stressful or traumatic, in the very moment it's happening, it could sometimes seem much too intense to experience or feel fully. There's this feeling that if you let yourself feel the thing you're afraid of fully feeling, you might be hurt or possibly even die," Gina continued.

"I see," I said, not entirely seeing but fascinated nonetheless, listening to see how this related to me.

Gina went back to her line of thought. "Above all, the role of the ego is to survive, at any cost. In order to survive, it needs to feel that it is in control. It needs certainty. When something happens that it can't control, it tries to find ways of dealing with it."

"So the ego's role is to survive. But the Indian *rishis* have told us, over and over, that the higher Self never dies, nor is it ever damaged by its experiences. Right?

So the ego is merely looking out for what it thinks is in danger." I tried to make sense of what little I had learnt so far about the higher Self and the ego.

"Well, yes, the ego or your identity, it's what enables us to act. It's the action hero in our spiritual journey. So it's an important character in our narrative as human beings. Sadly, the ego is fragile. It's terrified of being annihilated and it will do anything, absolutely anything, to avoid being killed off. It's a born survivor. So it looks for strategies to deal with whatever it feels threatens its survival." Gina sipped her wine.

"Like, deny the fact that you're feeling upset or that that something someone's done has hurt you?" I asked.

"Yes. Another example of a way you can rationalise is by blurring out or even deleting the event that caused you the trauma," she said. "Or by pushing it away or shutting out the feelings of guilt or sadness or anger or frustration or fear, or whatever. Suddenly you can't feel them, so they don't exist."

"So the ego just wants to look and feel good, at all times. It wants to be seen to be in control," I said. "Regardless of what lies inside, like cramming old or unwanted things in the garage instead of making an effort to clear away what you no longer need. Or stuffing rubbish in the storage space under the sofa seat or inside cupboards, or chucking it in the laundry basket instead of throwing it away in its rightful place." I tried to understand. "Is that what you mean by the ego pushes away and locks undesirable feelings into the back of the mind?"

"Exactly! Sooner or later, the smell of rotting rubbish that's stashed away will waft out. And the longer you leave these old traumas without dealing with them, being brutally honest about how they're impacting you in the present, the more they grip you," Gina said.

"By 'grip', do you mean that they drive how you feel and what you do? You're sort of a slave to all those unresolved feelings and emotions? So you're not really free to be yourself?" I asked.

Gina smiled. "What you resist persists—Carl Jung."

"So would that explain why I'm waking up with dread in my stomach lately? It's all those things that have happened over the years, with my mum, the furore caused by not getting married early, then being adamant about buying my own flat and leaving home. All the emotional upset that's built up around it?" I put my fork down and looked at her. "Would it be fair to call it emotional constipation? Because that's how I feel!" I said.

"That's not a bad way of putting it. Just as you need to fully digest and assimilate every meal, so you need to fully integrate your mental and emotional experiences because they impact your psychology." What Gina said made a lot of sense.

"I see. I'm emotionally constipated!" I said, moving my hand over my bloated belly. We both laughed. "So it's not a done deal at all. It continues to drive how I see things, whether I want to or not," I repeated, taking Gina's view on board. "So how can you know what issues are still lingering within you and how can you free yourself of them? Because what you're really saying is, that you cannot have any control or choice over yourself or your life when things that you don't know are driving you are running the show, isn't that so?" I asked as I started to see the relevance of what Gina was sharing with me.

"Precisely! If there is such a thing as being a master of your destiny, it needs you to become conscious of which stresses and traumas are still looping within you, however much in the background it might be. Psychologists say you can heal old traumas or as the Americans often say, bring 'closure' to these past issues."

Master of your destiny! I had come across these words a hundred times and cynically heard them as just a cliché. But today, these same words gave me goosepimples, as if I was hearing them for the first time. What if they were not just a cliché? Could I really be the master of my own destiny? What if I could? What would it take? And how would my life be different to merely being at the mercy of my *karma*? What if I could make friends with the Lords of *Karma*?

"The ancient Indian *rishis* talked about resolving *karma* or working out *karma* to complete its cycle," I pondered aloud. Little did I know that in the years to come, I would learn much more about 'karmic resolution', that my Inner Diamond would lead me to places far and wide to make such 'karmic resolution' possible.

"So how do you resolve such long-standing issues, that may sometimes stretch back over lifetimes, if what the *rishis* say is to be believed? That word, 'closure', seems to be trendy these days! But how do you really *bring* 'closure'?"

As I reflected upon these existential questions, I felt like there was a mountain for me to climb if I was ever going to be a master of my destiny.

"It's a process but, in a nutshell, you have to become consciously aware of what's really going on within you, acknowledge what the event was that triggered the trauma. And a trauma can be anything that aroused a strong emotional reaction in you. It could be a horrific event or it could be something insignificant," she said, and I could only nod, wanting her to tell me more.

She continued, "So, let's say that a boy of six gets excited when he passes by the sweet shop and he insists that he wants an ice lolly. His mum says no but the kid carries on asking for the ice lolly. His mum loses her patience and in her frustration, scolds him and emphatically tells him that he's not going to have that ice lolly. This seemingly insignificant event could be enough for the little boy, from the perspective of his mere six years, to leave him feeling unloved or unwanted. Nothing could be further from the truth, but if he really begins to believe that his mum doesn't want him or doesn't love him, then that becomes the truth for him. And from that moment on, something changes in him and when he doesn't get what he wants the next time, that feeling of being unloved or unwanted gets reinforced, fuelling the myth that he believes is his life."

As Gina explained this possible scenario, it began to dawn on me just how malleable our minds are.

"In *yogic* philosophy, the ancient *yogis* had clearly distinguished the layers of the mind. Yoga's Rishi Patanjali, in his *Yoga Sutras*, wrote about the core of human dilemma—the workings of the different layers of our own consciousness," Gina said.

"Really? Did you learn about that during your time in India with your mum?" I asked, fascinated.

"Yes, from hours and hours of lectures that seemed really boring at the time. Sage Patanjali, credited by many as being the Godfather of yoga, centred the entire philosophy and practice of *yoga* on this very theme. He taught that our consciousness, known as *citta*, has three parts."

"Really! How interesting," I said. "What are they?"

"He said that they were the mind, known as *manas*; self or ego, known as *ahamkara*; and intelligence, known as *buddhi*," Gina said. I listened in awe of her knowledge.

She continued, "I remember another one of my mum's amazing *yoga* teachers, a man called BKS Iyengar, comparing the mind or *manas* to the skeletal and muscular body that contains the internal organs. He said that the mind is, by its very nature, fickle and unsteady. Making productive choices is not its strong suit. It cannot discriminate between good and bad, right and wrong, accurate and inaccurate. It needs the inner layer of the intelligence or *buddhi* to do that. The self or ego, *ahamkara*, then presents itself as personalities or identities that represents the true Self."

"I see," I said, grappling with all these concepts. "But where, then, does this business of self-awareness come from, among these layers?"

"Good question," Gina answered. "According to these *yogic* sages, our consciousness, our capacity to be aware, lies beneath the mind. This can be awareness of the external world and the internal. It's that which *yogis* refer to as self-awareness." She smiled.

"Would you believe it if I told you that, after months and months, I'd finally gone to see my parents last weekend. Papa asked me to help me sort out his vast collection of books and one in particular got my attention. It was a book called *Light on Yoga* ...."

"By BKS Iyengar! I know it well," Gina said.

"Exactly. I brought it home with me but haven't read it yet. What a coincidence that you happen to be talking about this same guy." I marvelled at the synchronicity.

"Ah, you see. There are no accidents. It's time for you to learn about these things."

"I scanned the book through and remember one sentence in which he likens the mind to a lake." I took another drink. "He said something like how a still mind reflects the beauty of the Self or the soul or something. That really struck a chord in me."

"Isn't that beautiful?" Gina agreed. "The one that touched me when I was learning about these things, travelling around India with my mum during those Indian summers, is Patanjali's aphorism that says, 'movements and fluctuations of the mind that disturb our consciousness'. It's so simple yet so true."

Back in the Piazza, enjoying my second glass of Chablis, I tried to put into my own words what Gina had been saying. "So, in a nutshell, everything we've been talking about, it all comes back to becoming a master of your mind, right?" I said. Gina nodded, smiling. "Goodness! So what you're saying is that we can see an event with the limited wisdom, or even just false understanding, of a given situation and we can convince ourselves that what we believe is the truth. When, in reality, we just didn't have a broad enough perspective to understand it."

"Yes, that's one example of how you can end up with a trauma that shapes you and by simply becoming aware of it, you can free yourself of its unnecessarily negative impact. If that little boy could become aware of the fact that he was just being a little boy and his mum reacted from stress, and that she still loved him, he could see that it was just another insignificant event. While he was there at the time, it wasn't about him at all. His mum would have reacted in the same way with his dad or her best friend." She took another bite of pizza.

"Then of course, there are those things that happen that are significant, like, say, a five-year-old girl loses both her parents in a car crash. Or a woman gets raped. Or someone loses a leg in a bomb attack."

"Yeah, what about when real traumas arise from tragedies over which you may not have control. How can you possibly stop feeling its effects on you as a person and in your life, in general?" I asked, upset just thinking about such possibilities.

"Then it becomes even more important to get to the core of how these events have made you feel and what conclusions they have left you with. It's about accepting and owning our feelings, no matter how painful, rather than avoiding or deleting them," Gina said. "In the end, any introspection where you delve into an issue so that you can get to the bottom of how it limits you must ultimately be about freeing you from the limitation, so that you fulfil your potential and live to the max."

"The *rishis* said that if you can stay with and fully feel your experience, you've brought into full awareness the thing that you least want to or the thing that you most fear, and it will disappear forever in just one moment and you will transcend it, freeing you from its grip forever." I recollected having read this in one of the many ancient texts that cluttered my dad's vast collection of books.

"Yes. The *rishis* were all about liberation. They understood how the mind works and how it binds you," Gina sighed and rolled her eyes. "God, my mum made me sit cross-legged on the floor for hours and hours listening to those long, endless lectures of her Indian *gurus*."

"You say that, but these days, even though people in my culture seem to aspire to *moksha* or liberation of the soul so that it is no longer subject to the *karmic* cycle of birth and rebirth, it amazes me how little freedom you are actually allowed!" I despaired.

"You mean *moksha's* a romantic notion?" Gina asked.

"It's an ideal but the truth is, in everyday Indian society, taking yourself away from the herd to attend to your individual soul's calling is taboo! Absolute taboo!" I said, clearly still traumatised by my recent adventures.

"I can imagine that for a mere stub of a twenty-year-old to feel this intense desire for freedom can only be interpreted as a rebellious act. Liberation is strictly controlled." Gina captured my dilemma in just one sentence.

"Gosh, you've hit the nail on the head!" I exclaimed. To me, Gina was special in her ability to 'get' me and in her willingness to understand me.

In being understood, I suddenly felt free.

I continued, "I hadn't thought of it that way but it's true. For me, freedom isn't a nice-to-have, it's like the very air I breathe. I think I treasure it above anything else in life. And you know, it's not just about freedom to do things and be free to express myself. It's about a whole different level of inner freedom."

Gina smiled with satisfaction. "You know, you may not realise it, but you're on an unusual quest. I'm sure that you are about to set off on an adventure that will take you places, on the planet and in the spiritual realms, that neither of us know much about yet."

"All things you've told me inspire me beyond anything I know. Because I can now see that, with a bit of work, I can begin to set myself free from whatever constrains me from being all that I am. I don't have to be a victim of anything that's happened! And knowing that is the door to discovering who I am beneath, who I really am," I said, exhilarated. "From this moment on, I'm a victim no more!"

"You've got it!" Gina replied, delighted.

"But it's scary too. It feels like I have a massive climb up the Himalayas awaiting me," I cried, immediately plummeting into despair at the thought of embarking upon climbing a gigantic physiological and spiritual mountain.

"Great," Gina said, sounding almost American. "I'm so pleased you're inspired. Some people would find the prospect of going on a deep, inner search thoroughly depressing and would rather carry on just as they are, convincing themselves that they're as happy as they can be, even knowing things could be so much better. That's what makes you exceptional," Gina said, beaming, moved to tears. "But you'll face this challenge. And what's more, you'll win. You'll come out victorious."

I smiled, moved by Gina's sentiments. "Didn't someone say that suffering is only optional?" I laughed, trying to lighten the soppy mood.

"You're the kind of person for whom suffering through life is not an option. I think what you're beginning to realise is that you won't be happy pushing the unresolved under the carpet. It's not an option but a compulsion for you to live life being true to yourself," Gina said.

"You know, I suddenly see an image of the mighty Goddess Durga, who rides through the jungle fearlessly on her powerful tiger, slaying any demon that keeps her from moving forward in life," I said, looking into Covent Garden's Piazza.

"Well, that's the kind of courage you'll need to summon up on your journey," Gina concluded softly.

The evening light had softened, and generous shades of oranges, purples and blues stroked the twilight sky. My thoughts turned again to the bygone civilisations that had, over the ages, shared the very same sky that we were enjoying today. I could not help being in awe of the rich tapestry of life, of which we were but a tiny, yet not insignificant dot.

We ordered coffee and desserts.

"The rishis said that if
you can stay with
and fully feel your experience,
you've brought into full awareness
the thing that you least want to or
the thing that you most fear.
Then, it will disappear forever in
just one moment
and you will transcend it,
freeing you from its grip forever."

# 18

## Blessing and Curse

I asked some more about Gina's life in New York for a while but she brought the conversation back to what had led me to leave home.

"You know, it's fascinating what happens when people come to live in a country with an almost diametrically opposed culture to the one that they've grown up in. You're a good example of two diverse cultures colliding," Gina said.

"Hmmm ... I don't think of it in that way. I just take it all in my stride and zig-zag in and out of whoever I'm talking to. They're both ways of life I love being a part of," I replied.

"That's what's so special. I never heard you complain once. Was it a struggle to explain to your family, that you had set your heart on doing things differently to what they had wanted for you?" Gina asked.

"Well, in the Western culture, you're expected to date and have maybe several relationships, until you find the one that's right for you to settle down with. It's even okay for you to start having boyfriends while you're at school. The Western system is one of trial and error. Not so with us. When I said to my family I didn't want to get married yet, I'm sure some of them immediately thought that I was being corrupted by Western ways, maybe have boyfriends and mess around. We Indian girls are not supposed to have boyfriends, much less have more than one relationship. And if by some stroke of genius you happen to be in a relationship, and if your parents find out about it, then they would expect you to get married to that same guy. In some severe instances, I've known of cases where the dad and uncles tried to get the girl away from her boyfriend and coerce her to marry someone they chose for her," I said. "My family would never dream of using such force, mind," I added.

"Really? That's pretty strict! I would have thought that since Indians have been in the UK now since, how long is it?" she asked.

"Well, some people came in the '60s but there was a big tranche out of Uganda that came in the early '70s," I replied.

"1970s! Things might have changed now that we're in the early '90s? That's twenty years on," Gina looked baffled.

"You would think so, but certainly not yet. Maybe things will change in the future, maybe the next century will be different. If I had it my way, we would integrate the two cultures and adapt them to the best of both worlds. But you know how it is, you can't make an omelette without breaking eggs."

"That's really interesting. Some cultures completely cut themselves off from their roots after being away for a few years and that creates an identity crisis. In the case of your culture, you identify even more strongly with it," Gina said, sounding like the academic that she had become.

"Precisely!" I nodded. "I felt strongly that getting married so early was just not right for me. At first, I was fine about it, even excited, because I really liked my husband-to-be. But as the arrangements were being made, the reality dawned on me. I realised how little I really knew myself. So then how could I make someone else happy? I got a clear, gut intuition that I had first to discover who I was. And that was unheard of in my culture! Only people who became monks did that kind of nonsense. These types of questions were for renunciates and philosophers, not for a tender young bud of a flower! I mean, the question was already answered for me. The path was already set. A girl, even if she had two or three degrees, has to get married, have children and serve her family. Once she's married, she can work if her family allows it, but her primary duty is non-negotiable. That's the deal! Yet, my intuition kept on getting stronger, almost like a nagging epiphany—something I couldn't ignore. I had to do something about it. I knew that I had to listen to it but that would mean confronting my dad," I sighed.

"What did you say to him? How did you feel about approaching him?" she asked.

"I was terrified!"

Gina probed. "What were you terrified of?"

"Of being disowned." I remembered the fear, like it was happening now.

Gina laughed, thinking I was joking. "Surely that sort of thing doesn't still happen?"

"Oh yeah! We Indians party like it's 1099! The fact that we're at the early part of the '90s in the twentieth century makes little difference to a culture that's rooted deep in thousands of years of tradition." I felt resigned. "You see, my dad's an open-minded and forward-looking sort of a guy. When it was just down to him, I had a lot of freedom. As a teenager, I could get away with doing things that my other Indian friends couldn't. My parents never interfered with my choice of friends. I could see them anytime I wanted to. I went out to discos and on trips with my school and so on. I even had Saturday and summer jobs since I was fourteen. I could wear whatever I liked. I was allowed to make my own choices, and I made sure that I kept them within the bounds of what I knew would be acceptable. Still, I felt like a free spirit. I couldn't imagine being controlled and manipulated. But this time, it was a different story altogether. This wasn't something that my dad could keep to himself. "

"How so? After all, you live in London and you have the right to choose for yourself what to do with your life. I mean, your dad couldn't lock you up at home, could he?" Gina was evidently grappling with the intricate dynamics of my ancient culture.

I appreciated her taking such an interest because, for a Westerner, even one whose hippy mother had exposed her early in life to Indian spirituality and philosophies, it must have been difficult to appreciate how strongly deep-rooted traditions of thousands of years shaped, to differing degrees, whomever was born into it, often simply by osmosis. It was something you could not escape, regardless of how 'modern' you might have fancied your family to be. It had you, whether you were born and bred in London or New York, or Kampala or Nairobi, just as much as it did someone born in a little town in the middle of India.

"Gina, our cultures are like fire and ice! When you have to make a decision, you only have to think about yourself and maybe one or two other people. You see, in my culture, a person takes decisions on their own at their peril, and does it only if she's prepared to bear the wrath of the demons. You're not an individual island, you're part of a wider community. When I have to make a decision, I have to think about legions of people, many of whom I may never have met! In fact, I might never even get a say in some matters to do with my own life. Important decisions are made among senior family members and they jointly come to a consensus. That goes doubly so for something so important as marriage. Can you imagine that?" I took a sip of Chablis, and waited for Gina to process everything I'd just said.

"No, I can't imagine having to do that." Gina looked and sounded exasperated.

"Hmmm … In the Western culture, you can stand on your own two feet; it's actually expected of you. But in our culture, standing alone means being alone. By yourself, you're nobody. It means no support. It means complete rejection."

"I see. So you making up your mind about not wanting to get married at just twenty, about what you wanted for your life, that was utterly out of the question?"

"Exactly. The Indian culture pivots around the family unit and 'family' is not just your parents and siblings, it's the extended family, and that could sprawl far and wide to your parents' brothers and sisters, possibly even your grandparents' hoards of relatives living in India or in the Masai Mara in Kenya or wherever. Then there are the people in the broader community, and what they have to say matters even more. Let's say that even if my clan showed some understanding and lenience towards my wishes, others in the community wouldn't necessarily care to understand," I said.

"So, people who're not necessarily related you, even their opinions matter? That's harsh going," Gina frowned.

"Yep. See, in India, much like in royal families," I said, "when two people agree to get married, they don't just marry each other, it's a union of two communities. Once there's been even a verbal understanding that two families will join their children in marriage, you can't go back on your word, not without losing face and also your family's standing in the community."

"Then of course, your family becomes fodder for the wagging tongues of the community, whose respect you prize above all else. 'What will people say' drives so many decisions because 'family honour' and 'reputation' is prized above all else," Gina said, starting to understand. "But I remember you adored the guy you were supposed to marry? Didn't you two get on really well?"

"Yes, I did, absolutely. And I was twenty, for goodness sake! I was also flattered that he had chosen me. And he was an amazing guy. Any girl would have fallen in love with him. But what kind of a partner would I make when I had no clue who I was myself? I kept feeling this question, like a calling from deep within, echoing around in me, *who am I, who am I, who am I*? Even at just twenty, I knew that it was something that I simply couldn't ignore. But to find the answer to that question, I had to be free to search for my answers and I didn't feel that would be possible once I was married, with children and family," I said, the agony of my quandary still fresh.

"Gosh! Such wise inquiry for one so young. That's so rare," Gina said.

"There are times when I've been so connected to my Inner Diamond. In those times, I've just known that what I was feeling was so right, like this calling. So then my dilemma was, do I betray myself by not following my heart or do I sell my soul to please the people I loved? Do I stay true to my higher Self and trust that the bonds of blood and love would one day prove stronger and more authentic than flimsy opinions of the so-called community?"

Gina looked at me with admiration.

"My poor dad! He was lumbered with the gargantuan task of breaking the bad news to all those proud people, whose standards and values I was about to bring tumbling down. I still feel bad that I put him through that. I so wish I could have found a better way of doing it," I said, feeling the ache in my heart, and tears sprang to my eyes with deep regret. For the consternation I had caused my parents. For the disappointment I must have been to my grandmother, whose acceptance I yearned more than anything else. For the sadness I bore at being bereft from every member of my the family that I dearly loved.

"Don't be so hard on yourself, sweetie. I think you've been extraordinary in how you're going about your life. Tell me, were you the eldest of all your cousins?"

"Yes, why?" I asked, not sure how this was relevant.

"Well, there you go then," Gina grinned. "You could have been the deity of diplomacy herself but you wouldn't have succeeded in getting a fair hearing."

"What makes you say that?"

"Well, surely, if your family allowed you to do what you wanted, something so indulgent as 'follow your heart', then wouldn't that open the floodgates for the younger ones to do the same?"

"Er ... I suppose so," I stuttered, still not getting her point.

"So in their world, they had no choice. They had to be seen to be making an example of you." Gina's words cut through me like a shower of razor blades, the possibility of it devastating me. "My grandmother, my mum's mum, was a devout Catholic and she had fervent ideas about how she wanted to raise her children and how they should live their lives. When my mum, who was the oldest of six kids, at the age of nineteen told her that she wanted to go India to learn *yoga* and meditation and such like, all hell broke loose. She was afraid that if she let the eldest get out of hand, then she wouldn't be able to control the others. And for her, it was a double betrayal that a child of hers wanted to abandon Catholicism and follow some pagan religion."

"I can imagine that there could be that," I said thoughtfully.

"You see, Smita, you're a pioneer. I saw that the very first time I met you. You're cast of a different mould," Gina said.

"Am I? I'm not so sure. I'm a carbon copy of my dad. We share similar traits and temperament. And just because I want different things to what my elders might have thought for me doesn't make me a pioneer. I mean, I'm no Einstein or Mandela or Gandhi or even a Richard Branson."

"Maybe so. And yet, you're someone who has a tendency to original thinking and new ways of being. You somehow slipped the net of cultural conditioning that most people go through in their early life and so you have to find your own way."

I put my fork down in surprise. "But I don't go out of my way to do things differently. I mean, I would much rather just fit in and please the people who matter to me and be the shining star. That would be so much easier. I don't want to invoke the wrath of demons every time I have to make a decision," I sighed.

"Yes, it would be easier to do things the traditional or more acceptable way—the way it pleases others. But beat yourself up as you might, but you know, there's no guarantee that even then you would succeed in being accepted. I'm sure there would have been some other reason, like someone didn't like your hairstyle and that was reason enough to exclude you. Or at work, a colleague told the others that they should not listen to you or do the things that you do because he was jealous of you. There are countless dynamics that determine how people treat you. Lots of things determine the extent to which you're accepted or rejected, and many of them may have nothing at all to do with what you did or said and everything to do with people's own perspective. So please, sweetie, don't be so hard on yourself."

Gina had a point.

Covent Garden Piazza was now in full swing, with people drinking, eating, laughing, and deep in conversation with their companions.

Gina continued with her reasoning. "There are times in history when the way things have been done until now become redundant or at least, need to be done differently because times have changed. In your case, it's because you have become a product of two very different cultures and you need a new model inside of which you can find your fulfilment."

"That's so true. If I agreed to do some of things the way I am expected to do them, well I'd just feel suffocated! I could just shut up and do it anyway but that's a sure recipe for me to be miserable. Utterly miserable! You know, Gina, to me, it occurred like I was selling out on myself, like I'm selling my soul to please others, so that I will be accepted or sometimes, just to avoid rejection. But being miserable is a high price to pay. I love nothing more than to please people but not when I deeply disagree with what's being asked of me. That I cannot do! I have no choice but to find my own way."

"There you go. You're a pioneer! Pioneers, by definition, are non-conformist," Gina said.

"But I'm not deliberately going out to not conform."

"Ah, pioneers don't seek to deliberately not conform, and neither do they deliberately seek out conflict. They have an innate sense of what's right for them. Whereas a conformist will look to the norm to define what to do, a pioneer will look elsewhere. Usually they look within themselves, for what's right and wrong. You see, they have a rare connection to their inner core, what you call your Inner Diamond, and that's their guide, not cultural norms or traditions." Gina smiled and leaned back in her chair. "It's just that conforming is simply not an option for them. They're more prepared to face the consequences than pay the high price of conformity that suffocates them."

"Maybe, but it's not like I go out to embrace having to do things differently. I mean, every single time, it terrifies me," I said, present to how excruciating the pain was each time I did something that was out of the norm.

"Pioneers may well be terrified of taking the action that they intuitively know they have to take, but they will take it anyway, even knowing there will be consequences," Gina said. "But they're willing to bear the consequences in service of being true to themselves. They're what you might call 'reluctant rebels'. They're not seeking deliberate conflict but they'll not shy away from confrontation either."

"So, being a pioneer is that state? Something that's innate and inherent within you?" I questioned.

"Yes, exactly. You're someone who doesn't need someone else to have done something before you to try it. You see the vision or the possibility, and you take it up and run with it. You don't have a conversation going on that no one has done it before whereas most people will only do things when others have done it."

"I see. Well, that does sound like me. So are pioneers entrepreneurs?" I said, relaxing my resistance.

"Not all entrepreneurs are pioneers but a lot are pioneers and they start something that no one has done before. By definition, a pioneer is a visionary. You can see the vision even if the thing itself hasn't yet come into existence. That's either because you dreamt it up yourself or because someone else showed it to you. Either way, you have what it takes to nurture the vision and bring it into existence," Gina said.

"Gina, you've blown my mind! It'll be one hell of a job to piece it together now," I said, deeply grateful for this life-altering exchange.

"That's a blessing and a curse at the same time. You're blessed because you're in touch with that rich, authentic, inner core. It's a blessing because not many people are born with that inherent awareness. But the curse is that you have had to, and you will again and again have to, make heart-wrenching choices in life. It's a curse because you may not be understood by those people around you whose understanding you might crave." As Gina spoke, I felt the click of our minds connecting and I realised that Gina, too, was a pioneer and that is why she understood me so well.

"You're beating yourself up for something that you just have to learn to accept," she continued.

"How do you mean?" I queried.

"Well, pioneers are people who have an inherent drive, a compelling pull if you like, to be true to that which is calling them and if they don't, their life just doesn't work. They fall sick or get depressed or something else happens that gets in the way of being in the flow. It all falls apart. You must learn to take responsibility for the way you are designed so that you can be free to be yourself."

I argued, "But isn't that the case of each one of us? I don't think I'm so special."

"Yes, that's true, but it's absolutely true for the way you are put together," Gina responded. "We each need to learn who we are and take responsibility for that because that's key to making the choices that are right for us as individuals. That's the difference between a person who's fulfilled in life and one who's constantly complaining and suffering. The difference? Most people consider it an option, a luxury, to take the time to understand ourselves, even though actually, it's not a luxury. It's essential. But the way you're designed, your natural inclination is to follow your heart. So it will really serve you well to know that you're ahead of your time and therefore, it's in your nature to be pulled towards doing things that others won't think are normal until maybe fifteen, twenty or twenty-five years later."

Gina had 'got' me. At last, I felt understood and though Gina was sitting across the table from me, her ability to capture my world felt like a warm, tender embrace enveloping me, healing the wounds from self-reproach for not fitting in, not even when I tried my hardest. It was the soothing balm that I needed to begin dissolving the guilt I felt, for being 'wrong'.

Even in the dreaded traffic of the City of London, I had a habit of driving everywhere. After finishing our desserts and coffee, I insisted on giving Gina a lift to her flat in Marylebone, where she was staying temporarily after returning from New York, until she found a more permanent place.

As Gina was getting out of the car, she suddenly exclaimed, "Oh, I nearly forgot!" and handed me a paper gift bag. "There's a book in here that I'd love for you to read. A friend gave me a copy to welcome me to New York and I knew I had to get the same for you. I loved this book! It puts you in touch with your inner core, that Inner Diamond of yours that you're always going on about. It also inspired me to start meditating. Beautiful and to the point, the messages are simply put, so don't let that intellectual brain of yours be put off by it. It's *anything* but easy to master."

I looked at the gift bag containing the book, which was wrapped in pink tissue paper. "Thank you. You're such a sweetie!" I said. "I'll open it later."

I was moved by Gina's affection for me. Given the age difference between us, it wasn't an obvious friendship and yet, it was very real and one that I cherished. I couldn't help adoring her. She, for the moment, was my one and only rock. I do not know what I would have done without her.

# 19

## Letting Go

That conversation with Gina had been like a rocket blasting open my inner world. She was truly playing the role of an angel in my life.

I had left home to grant myself freedom, and yet I was a long way from being free within. The galactic space that had opened up within me felt just as unnerving as it did exciting. Soon, this new way of being became normal and I felt more settled and secure. A new calm entered my solitude. In the stillness of my new environment, an irreversible healing had begun. It was the kind of healing that, over the years to come, would break up and turn the entire fabric of my being upside down and inside out. My transformation was underway.

I'd rocked a lot of boats and upset many people. Had left home racked with guilt, which slept like a coiled serpent within me. It was as if this serpent was caught up in the net of a curse that had me bound in its spell, to forever feel every inch that troublesome outsider that I feared my elders doomed me to be. It was as if I had been given a life sentence: I am not worthy, I do not deserve the good that life has to offer.

With that loop running and re-running of its own will in my mental background, it was no wonder that sadness continued to engulf me, strangling any possibility of happiness. Regardless, I was not willing to be a victim of my feelings, nor of my past, for the rest of my life. Neither did I want to suppress them and carry on pretending to myself that everything was 'fine'—that I was 'fine'. If there was one thing that my conversation with Gina had highlighted, it was that I was anything but fine. Something had to be done and I had to do it now.

The week after I had met Gina in Covent Garden, I decided to free up an hour after coming home from work to allow space for these feelings of melancholy to surface, in the safe and peaceful environment of my home. Maybe, I thought, if I could just sit with whatever was going on for even only a few minutes a day and look it in the eye, as it were, it would run its course, just like a ball of wool eventually runs out. Rather than run away from my wounded, vulnerable self, I had made up my mind to befriend it, let it be, give it air and light, and put my faith in the knowing that I had heard many times: all things must eventually pass, and this too shall pass.

Every day after work, I came home, lit a *ghee* butter lamp and a stick of my favourite jasmine incense, mentally offering them up to the generous Lord Ganesh, or sometimes to Shiva, the *yogi* of all *yogis*, or to the mighty Goddess Durga. I would close my eyes and take in several deep breaths, then put out a prayer from the depths of my being. *Please free me from the prison of my own pain and anguish. Let me be light and joyful. Let me be whole and see beyond myself. Connect me to my Inner Diamond again. Free me and use me to serve others.* This fragrant little ritual, though simple, I hoped would drift me into an inner space of calm and silence.

For the first few evenings that I sat down to meditate, I realised just how restless my mind was— its clutter virtually impenetrable. Whereas I expected the silence to drop me into an experience of peace and stillness, it seemed to do the opposite; it stirred up the debris that perhaps had been rotting in the dark shadows that lurked beneath my conscious mind: disappointments, fears and the very pain and anguish from which I sought to be free.

Every time I closed my eyes and let my breath settle, the commentary of a judgemental little voice in my head ran rampant—I started calling it my inner critic. It hijacked my thoughts with its loud and unruly rebukes. *See what you've done? Lost on your own, aren't you? I told you*

*you'd be miserable. And alone! You can't make it on your own, can you? You're too weak. You're just trouble! You'll never be happy! No Indian man will ever want to marry you, now that you're 'svatantra' (independent)! You'd better make a success of yourself otherwise you're up a creek without a paddle!* And so it went on and on, stirring up even more fear.

The deeper my mind went into silence, the louder the inner critic's rantings became. I had no idea that the little voice in my head was so utterly powerful, scathing, and debilitating. I was a beginner at meditating and had no facility yet with bringing myself back when my mind wandered into dark nooks and crannies of negativity. I could not help being gripped by the inner critic's commentary. Where did it come from? Who put it there? How much of it was there? This carried on every day for about two weeks. I just watched these thoughts arise and with them, bring up all manner of aches and pains and fear in different parts of my body.

Wasn't the purpose of meditating to calm the mind, to quieten this very noise? Then why had it become louder instead of quietening down? Why did I feel more restless?

There had to be more to this meditation lark than this! Otherwise why did people do it? Why did my dad sit in meditation for what seemed to me like hours and hours and hours, ever since I could remember? I persisted with it for a few minutes every day, even if on some days I felt more hopeless than when I had started.

After about two weeks, I wondered if I was doing it wrong and wasting my time. The little voice in my head was so vociferous that I could hear nothing else but its commentary, and it affected my confidence at work and made me even more miserable.

In the third week, after lighting the *ghee* lamp and incense, I tried connecting with my Inner Diamond to ask for its counsel. I asked: Am I doing this meditation lark correctly? Tell me how to do it.

No sooner had I asked the question than I felt the urge to get up and go to my bedroom. The first thing my eyes fell on upon entering the room was Gina's gift bag, with her present still wrapped in pink tissue. Having come home late that night after seeing her, I had left it unopened under my dressing table, out of everyday sight, and forgotten all about it, until now. I unwrapped the tissue paper to find a paperback book. It was a book about connecting with the higher Self. Though I had connected with the Inner Diamond on occasions, it had sort of just happened, accidentally or by chance or pure luck. If you asked me how to do it, I could not explain it. Just knowing that someone else out there believed that it was possible to connect with the higher Self, and that they might have a method for doing it, intrigued me.

Back on the sofa of my living room, I thumbed through the pages, devouring the words that leapt off the page as if they had some magic woven into them. As Gina had said, for such an esoteric, elusive subject, this book was easy to read. It had an ethereal quality about it and was packed with grounded, clear messages, exercises, and visualised meditations to help you connect with the higher Self—the Inner Diamond. It was as if it had been written to remind you what you already knew but was buried in the layers of ancient memory.

Then, I came across a chapter about how to first observe and then let go of negative feelings, emotions and beliefs that hampered you from being happy or successful, and other states of being that we all secretly hold hope for. Having let go of the limiting negative thoughts, the next chapter gave instructions about how to inspire powerful, positive perspectives and articulate them in a way that would help you to bring into reality whatever you put your mind to. There was also a visualised meditation that took you through this process.

I started to work with the visualisation process but, as soon as my mind quietened down, instead of using the steps given in the book, I sensed the presence of my Inner Diamond and it took me on an inner guided journey. The book had said to take the thoughts, memories or feelings that were the most difficult in that moment and work with those. That was easy. I felt painfully rejected, unaccepted, and excluded as the black sheep that I had become.

*"Imagine that you are holding every one of those thoughts, feelings and memories in your hands,"* my Inner Diamond guided gently, having taken the form of a beautiful woman draped in a gossamer white *sari*, delicately woven with embroidery of tiny pearls and diamonds that glistened in the luminescent light that enveloped her white opal wings.

I learnt later that the higher Self is formless and it exists everywhere and nowhere, making it much too abstract as a concept to 'connect' with. It therefore helps to visualise it having a form that we can relate to. So instead of my higher Self showing up as a beautiful demi-angel, she could just as well have taken the form of a fierce, hairy Hell's Angel with tattoos of blood-soaked vampires and riding a Harley Davidson, or even a blood-soaked vampire itself riding a bat from hell—only, in my personal frame of reference, that would not have been a very comforting prospect.

*"Place all those thoughts and feelings into an object that you can hold in your hand,"* the angelic form of the higher Self said.

I did so, visualising a red apple, and every one of my thoughts and excruciating feelings of being rejected and unwanted, of being a burden, streamed out of my solar plexus and into the fruit. The apple turned more and more rotten with the negativity it contained until I couldn't hold it in my hand any longer.

The luminous angel took the rotten apple from my hand and flicked it up, as if she were playing divine cricket or baseball, and it transmuted into a ball of orange light, disappearing into the golden glow of the sun. I visualised my negativity pouring out of me, into new red apples, until nothing more was left, at least as far as my feelings of rejection were concerned.

*"Now what else don't you want to hold on to anymore?"* she asked, digging her index finger of light into the right side of my heart. As she did so, it triggered a series of painful, stunted thoughts that released into a stream of consciousness in my mind. I caught each one, like a burnt leaf floating off a tree in an autumn gust: I mustn't be a burden, I'm trouble, I'm difficult. And so they carried on flowing. I caught each thought in my hand as if it were a dry, brown autumn leaf, and the

glowing angelic form of my higher Self picked each leaf from between my fingers, once again transmuting it into multi-coloured luminous shapes that escaped into the light above.

When I had no more negative thoughts that I could muster up, she pointed to a beautiful dazzling glow of lilac, violet, purple, and orange—much like the colours of the sunset Gina and I had seen over Covent Garden some weeks ago, only now, the colours were a thousand times sharper, more vibrant. The glow undulated, like flames of a purple fire. She asked me to step with her into the centre of this purple fire and said, *"Look to the future and choose a new reality. Create powerful, positive beliefs that will make your life joyful and abundant."* Her eyes sparkled. Then, taking my hands into hers, she said, *"Learn to think in inspired ways that serve to make your life a masterpiece of art!"* The beauty of this higher consciousness, this mere thought, set me ablaze with inspiration.

She placed her index finger, the finger of light, on my heart, making it feel like a vibrant balloon of joy. I could have burst there and then but I had to be present, to choose new thoughts and beliefs that would be worthy of such a boon, to *feel* myself into a new reality. At first, doing so felt phoney and ridiculous. I could hear the jibes of my inner critic again. *You're so pathetic!* I hesitated, holding back my mind from coming up with anything.

*"Your mind is the most powerful tool you have,"* my higher Self said gently. *"Learn to use it wisely."*

I realised that my mind was being judgemental about this process. The very next realisation was that this was one of the ego's tactics of staying in limited thinking. The mind was capable of so much more, as my higher Self said, than what you enable it to be and even if this process felt simplistic and somewhat whimsical to my ego, I was going to try on the counsel of my Inner Diamond.

Then my higher Self said, *"Remember that the ego likes confusion. It thrives on making what is simple into something complicated. It likes to feel clever."*

"Why?" I asked her, confused, and then realised that this was my ego asking the question.

*"Because that's how it keeps itself alive,"* my higher Self replied, her words carefully chosen.

*"Every thought and belief is real only for so long as you energise it by giving it power over you."*

"But what about the feelings and emotions that go with these thoughts? They don't just go away, do they?" I asked. My ego was still resisting.

*"Not at first. But with time, they too will blur and fade away."* She placed a hand on my head.

Warmth oozed into my brain and down my spine, into the branches and tributaries of my nervous system, awakening me a little more into a new reality. As I stood in the midst of the giant purple fire, my higher Self transmitted this energy and understanding into my conscious mind, and I noticed a new stream of thoughts arising. *I am worthy of love. I deserve the best of life. I deserve success.*

With these sentiments, a surge of forgiveness and gratitude welled up within me. I asked forgiveness of my parents and grandparents for not being the daughter they might have wanted me to be. I asked for forgiveness of all my family for disappointing them in not doing things their way. I found myself forgiving them for not understanding me. I even began to accept myself for being 'different'. Then my heart filled with overwhelming gratitude for this moment, for getting the precious connection back with my Inner Diamond, for all the love, laughter and togetherness that I'd enjoyed over the years with my family. A deep gratitude welled up for my grandmother for lovingly raising me, and that my mother was now well.

"I choose love, laughter and joy. I choose abundance and I choose to be fully alive," I said, soaking up the intrinsic peace that this experience had brought about in my mind, body and soul.

# 20

# Beneath an Ancient Banyan Tree

Over the coming days, every evening, I performed the same ritual of lighting the *ghee* butter lamp and incense. On some days, my concentration and connection was stronger than on others. Every day my experience of the practice was different. I would have expected my meditation to be deeper when I felt calm and centred but instead, long forgotten memories and associated stresses or traumas, big or small, surfaced spontaneously and, like moths to light, sizzled away into nothingness. Yet on other days, quite unexpectedly, I could slip deep into the stillness of consciousness and, just as spontaneously, the gaps between thoughts would extend into pure silence, making time as fluid as the ocean.

On one occasion, I found myself floating back in time, I could not say exactly how far back, but it was certainly a few hundred years, if not a thousand or more. In what looked to me like a village in old India, I saw a *yogi*—a nearly naked man dressed only in a loincloth, sitting cross-legged in perfect Lotus posture. He sat deep in meditation beneath an ancient banyan tree, with trailing tresses that dangled around his face and still body. His matted, long dreadlocks, crowned a thin, chiselled face, and fell below his shoulders—his fair but tanned Indian skin radiant, and saturated with a glow that perhaps came from his smooth, silent breath.

Still aware that I was in my meditation, I merely observed him from a distance for a while, mesmerised by his stillness and total absorption of focus. What was he seeing? What was he feeling? What was his experience, deep in meditation? Then, as I observed long enough, I spiralled across time and space into his time. He, as though he were aware of my presence, invited me through a silent mental or spiritual connection into his world. I felt myself pulled into his being, then becoming him, and our individual boundaries merged, our meditations collapsed together, and our respective times and space converged as we became one-and-the same person.

Were he and I the same? Was I merely remembering another incarnation as that *yogi* in ancient India in a previous life? In that merged state, I could not tell and neither did I care, though I certainly fancied the notion that I had tapped into memories of a previous life. From inside of his consciousness, I was able to see and feel what he was seeing and feeling: an expanded state of awareness that transcended time and space, where there was only the present moment. Being one with the present moment, with nowhere to get and only the incoming and outgoing breath for sustenance, this *yogi* felt completely nourished and content.

As that *yogi*, I could extend, through the medium of consciousness, into all experiences I ever had and would ever know in the future. In this state of being merged, one with another, the veils of illusion blew away and flew across the ocean of time to meet somewhere in the space of timelessness.

Whether that *yogi* was me in a previous lifetime or not, I was now certain that I had learnt to meditate before this lifetime and that it was second nature to me. Though it would take me some years to remember how to work its magic, I had somehow stumbled upon one of my most inherent abilities and one that had creaked open the door to the mystical, pure brilliance that I called my Inner Diamond—which, I would later learn, the sages of ancient India called *Atman*.

"You see, you are a brilliant,
sparkling diamond...
this is who you are.
When you will know yourself as this,
the innermost truth of who you are,
you will not just have 'fun', but
that becomes your innate state...
You will be 'fun', in its highest octave."

# 21

## Going Within

**M**editation quickly became a central pillar in my life and I practised it religiously over the next three years. I used visualisation journeys as a tool for creating the future, where I could consciously allow it to unfold from within the vision of what my Inner Diamond wanted to bring forth into my life, as opposed to goals and mere desires driven by my ego. This gave me a profound sense of being in collaboration with the Diamond's higher wisdom. The power of these visualisations was that they brought to life in my mind's eye that which I was 'creating' in such a palpable way that I could not just see it, but sense it and even almost taste it. The trick was to feel its essence and its qualities: the way it made me feel. So when money was being shown to me, it was not so much the money itself, but letting myself feel the emotional and mental state of what money facilitated. Intuitively, I soaked up the energy of Goddess Lakshmi, the deity of wealth and good fortune, so intensely that, in that moment, even without the wealth I was being shown, it left me feeling deeply satisfied, joyful, and happy.

In this way, the whole process of manifesting became tangible, making me irresistible to the thing I wanted to make happen in my life. Another value of the visualisation process was that it brought to life the maxim 'you'll believe it when you see it'. Seeing it with my third eye or the mind's eye tricked the subconscious mind into thinking that it was already real, thereby triggering the process of making it happen in material reality.

I asked my Inner Diamond to show me that which would be for the highest good in the area of my work too, to help me be crystal clear about what I could accomplish and by when. So, for example, win two new customers who would bring in a specific sum of business by a certain date. The important thing about the process was to focus on how it would make me feel when I had this happen—for example, experiencing delight or exhilaration or peace or fulfilled and so on. Always, I chose for things to come to me easily, effortlessly and joyfully because while I enjoyed throwing myself into my work and worked hard, I certainly did not want working hard to seem like hard work.

In these visualised meditations, my Diamond showed me how to work with objects, symbols and patterns of light to represent what I wanted to create: one picture told the story of a thousand words. This was a new way of doing things for me and it energised me with inspiration. More and more, I tapped into my intuition to know whether it was the right time to get in touch with my customers, when best to call for their response to a proposal, whether to talk about a particular proposition and so on. As I strengthened my connection to my Inner Diamond and paid attention to its nudges through my intuition, I started to produce exceptional results at work. I was working harder than before, but also enjoyed it more than ever and, despite working hard, like falling off a log, there was an ease about it.

The right man still eluded me though. Being single meant I had plenty of time on my hands outside of work. It left me free to learn about and get qualifications in all kinds of healing arts such as different kinds of massage and reflexology. I even designed a collection of clothes that fused Indian traditional styles and fabrics with Western cuts. During my holidays from work, I made flying visits to different parts of India to find the exact type of silk fabrics I had in mind for my collection. Then I invested in hiring a professional pattern cutter to make patterns or my designs so that I could have the garments stitched in India by tailors introduced to me by family friends. My real expertise was selling and I was surprised how easy it was to convince the buyers of the upmarket stores, Harrods and Fenwick in New Bond Street, to sell my collection.

Despite my accomplishments at work and surprising success even in my hobbies, something remained missing. Meditation had allowed so much of my sadness and anger to surface and, in the light of conscious awareness, dissolved them for good. The dark clouds of heaviness that had followed me when leaving home were evaporating too, and in so doing opened up more inner spaciousness. Enough emotional debris must have cleared away that I could hear the whisperings of 'there's something more'. It was not something that I could achieve or earn my way out of, but something that I had spontaneously stumbled upon through the cracks between the silence of my meditation practise.

These whisperings grew louder and louder into a longing over the course of the next year, drowning out the satisfaction I had been enjoying in my work life. The longing became a loud, not to be ignored call, to which I felt compelled to respond. I felt called to meditate longer and deeper, as if there was a pot of gold, some kind of knowledge, to dip into.

It was a yearning for something mystical but I had I no idea what that looked like.

# 22

# The Calling

In the space created by the healing of old wounds, I became aware of deeper stirrings in my consciousness that brought to my attention a sense of longing for something more than what I knew my life to be. Aside of the longing were many questions.

Working and socialising now and then, was that all my life was for? What was this longing for 'something more'? What was this 'something more' anyway? Was it a call to something significant? Or was I just looking for an escape? How could I make my life count for something? How could I use it to somehow be more meaningful? Why did I have this odd yet familiar desire, like going into the mountains and meditating, maybe permanently, as if it was the most natural thing to do...?

With so many questions, and now that I could again hear its counsel and intuitive inklings, I turned once more to my Inner Diamond. One evening, settling into my meditation practice, not quite knowing exactly which question to ask first, I let rip my stream of consciousness. I enquired inwardly to the Diamond.

My thoughts cut off in mid-sentence, and I sat up, startled by the loud roaring reply, *"It is not for you this time to go off into the hills and disappear from the world!"*

Could that be my gentle Inner Diamond? My Diamond's rare roar startled me out of my meditation. I opened my eyes and looked around the room to see in case there was someone physically present in the room with me. It wasn't often that the Diamond responded so emphatically and with such passion and directness. It took me a moment or two to grasp that the boom I'd heard was indeed my Diamond responding. After absorbing the shock of its response, I collected myself and asked, "'This time'? I've never been to meditate in the mountains, have I?"

*"Yes, you have, many times you have given up worldly life in search of your Self. That was fine then, but this time, you came here to take on a challenge: the challenge of integrating two worlds—the spiritual with the material, the inner with the outer."*

I remained silent for a while, absorbing what my Inner Diamond was now revealing to me.

"That sounds like a tall, no, a soaring order! Has anyone succeeded in doing that yet? And why me?" I asked, not knowing whether to interpret this as a life-sentence, and panic, or to let excitement grip me.

*"If you are to experience inner freedom in this lifetime, you must go back into some of your past lives and resolve incomplete issues that are blocking you even today. When you have seen your past, you will then understand 'why you?' and why you can."*

"How on earth am I going to do that? How does one find past lives anyway? And how do you know which ones to go for?" I asked.

*"Trust and take action. Stay tuned. Keep listening and all will be revealed, one step at a time."*

I stayed silent for a while, wondering if I was going completely cuckoo.

"Okay. So what do I do now?"

*"Go back to India for six months. This time, travel and learn from the holy ones and be healed in their presence."*

I couldn't help being panic-stricken. "But, hang on! How could I possibly do that? I have a mortgage to pay and hardly enough saved to cover the bills *and* hang around for six months in India!" I felt almost hysterical, and well and truly out of my meditative calm. This was not how meditation was supposed to be.

What on earth was my crazy Diamond calling me to do now? And what did it mean, 'integrating two worlds, the spiritual with the material'? How was that feasible? Was that even possible? If so, why had those wise old sages not told us how to do this? And if they had, I certainly didn't know about it.

*"You will have the money,"* my higher Self's voice assured me through my inner ear.

"How? I'm not going to sell this flat, if that's what you want me to do." Although I argued, my thoughts fell down an abyss. There was no answer. Frustrated, I got up, abandoning my meditation.

Shortly afterwards, I made myself dinner and, just as I was sitting down to eat, I heard a clamour coming from down the stairs. It was the banging of my metal letterbox. I went to answer the door, thinking it was probably the pizza delivery guy knocking on my door instead of my neighbour's. There was no one there— only a free marketing leaflet which had been stuffed crudely in my letterbox. Annoyed at the mindless intrusion, I pulled the leaflet out and glanced at it as I walked back up the stairs. It was from the local estate agent. "We are urgently looking for properties like yours to lease to our new corporate clients. Minimum six months let ... Generous rental returns guaranteed ...

We will fully manage your property for your peace of mind."

Go to India for six months, my Diamond had ordained. Of course! I twigged, I could rent my flat for six months. That would solve my dilemma. I smiled. Hadn't the Diamond just told me to trust and I would find the money? I felt silly for not coming up with that idea myself, and yet, this solution was far from something I would have considered as an option. Still, even after seeing this, I went around for days with my head in a nozzle, wondering where in India to go, who to see, and where to begin such a vague quest.

A few days later, during one of my meditations, the Diamond suddenly popped up again. *You've been worrying for days. Let go of the fear. I will guide you. I am your compass."*

Just as it said that, it occurred to me that maybe a safe place to start was to go and see my family in Ahmedabad and take it from there.

Even so, this was all too radical, even for me. The guidance of my higher Self was to drop everything and go and find myself in India. Alone. Anyone who knew anything about India surely knew one thing: it is not a place designed for a young woman to travel on her own.

I realised more and more that engaging with the Inner Diamond was no joke. When you asked it to bring you your joy, it would not fail. However, how it brought it to you and what it might call on you to give up and let go of, try as you might, you could not anticipate in advance. And your ego may not like what it would ask you to do next.

A life guided by the Inner Diamond was, for certain, one thing: full of surprises.

No wonder people stayed far away from connecting to the higher Self. If you listened to it, really listened to it, it could take you far, far out of your comfort zone and well away from who you 'knew' yourself to be.

That said, it would never fail you, provided you stayed the course.

Collaborating with the higher Self meant heeding its call and doing so with commitment and inspired action. To put so much trust in the Inner Diamond felt scary, but I also knew that I would not be disappointed.

I had two choices. I could stay as I was and stagnate, or I could respond to the call for the quest, a veritable adventure, and choose with my heart and soul to trust in my Inner Diamond. After all, it had always shown up for me in my moments of need and carried me this far.

My choice was made.

My tickets to India, booked.

Quite apart from having all my questions answered, my journey had only just begun.

# About the Author

Born in the port town of Porbandar in Gujarat, India, my parents and I moved to London when I was ten. I studied in England, undertaking English, French and Politics at college. In a career spanning 25 years, I took on increasingly challenging responsibilities in the corporate world. One of my main roles was selling multimillion-dollar contracts into well-known global companies. Through the business I was in, I'm proud to have been one of the pioneers bringing India's Information Technology services into the heart of British and European companies.

Alongside my corporate career, I became a life coach and led personal transformation programmes to groups of hundreds at a time. As a freelance TV presenter, I interview *gurus*, entrepreneurs and politicians. A devoted practitioner, I'm also a certified *yoga* instructor.

I'm married and live in London.

## Behind the Author

My birth town of Porbandar, a buzzing port along North West India's Arabian Sea coastline, is better known as the home of Mahatma Gandhi. I was brought up in a traditional Indian home with values rooted in ancient Vedic culture. We lived for most of my childhood close by the sea and some of my years were spent in a beautiful sea-facing house of my grandad's, a well-respected lawyer. As with many children in India, I was fortunate to have the influence of a grandmother who imbued in me the values of the age-old culture into which I was born. She encouraged me to read daily the Bhagavad Gita in Gujarati and to recite various Sanskrit *mantras* before I'd turned seven. This gave me a solid foundation on which to later build as I strived to heal the traumas of my past, and bring balance to a hectic life while working as a business executive with large global companies.

I loved my life in London and its flourishing entrepreneurial culture. Like a duck to water, I thrived on working internationally in hardcore business environments, selling leading-edge technology contracts to multi-national corporations. I am proud to have been one of the pioneers to convince large Western companies to start working with the Indian IT industry, which was growing in those days from its infancy into one of the largest parts of the Indian economy.

But at the same time, while working in the cut-throat world of business, I was fascinated by who we are deeper within. It was not long before I felt compelled to balance my professional corporate existence with, at the same time, finding a way to nourish my soul.

I yearned to experience more of the soulful, radiant inner being that I had seen glimpses of at various times in my life. During my holidays and sabbaticals, I travelled across India with *yogis* and *gurus* to see what more I could discover about the Self within. I pored over the Vedas, Bhagavad Gita, Shiva Sutras, the Puranas and Upanishads, soaking up whatever I could and went about applying some of these teachings to improve my quality of life, including in my work. Later in my quest, I travelled to many other places, including New Mexico, Hawaii and Kauai to seek out special people, places and answers to unresolved questions that throttled the possibility that life offered.

As my self-awareness grew, so did my desire to serve others. Alongside of my business life, when not travelling for work or meeting deadlines, I dedicated my weekends, holidays and any spare time over a number of years to become a life coach. I first followed a few years of hard training on how to help others in a responsible way to uncover their deepest issues and transform themselves. Then, I was allowed to go and assist in such programmes. It was not long before I had the privilege of leading these cutting-edge series of workshops myself, coaching large groups of 100 - 300 people at a time on how to deal more powerfully with the challenges of modern life and realise their goals and aspirations.

## Yoga - the context for my life

As a child, I grew up watching my father regularly stand on his head for what seemed to me like hours. He was doing the Shirasana *yoga* posture. Guided by his *guru*, the brilliant Sri Aurobindo, my father was an avid *yogi* who meditated regularly. Though Dad never taught me directly, simply watching him stand stock-still on his head and sit statuesque in deep, meditative immersions, captivated my imagination as a little girl. Around the age of twelve, I too started to attempt performing *yoga* postures. A few years later, I also began to meditate, purely guided by my intuitive inklings. On and off, I did *yoga* for twenty years but it was only when I stumbled into my first Vinyasa Flow training course did my *yoga* practise begin in earnest. This was with the extraordinary, internationally renowned *yoga* teacher, Shiva Rea. Her profound knowledge and approach to integrating the different aspects of *yoga* touched me deeply and inspired by Shiva, I took up training with her to be able to teach.

Other accomplished *yoga* masters of the Krishnamacharya lineage with whom I have studied include David Swenson, Richard Freeman, Ana Forrest, Anna Ashby, Hamish Hendry and Stewart Gilchrist. As well as Shiva Rea's Prana Flow Yoga, I also practise Mysore Style Ashtanga and other forms of dynamic yoga. I teach regularly and am committed to my daily practice.

## Diving Deep

People and cultures fascinate me and I love exploring different parts of the world. My love of travel has taken me to swim with wild dolphins, exploring volcanoes, and visit temples, shrines and mystical places across the world.

I've studied several Indian and Buddhist spiritual systems and continue to delve into their richness to discover new facets of who we are. Unveiling the mysteries of the mind, spirit and what it means to be human excites me.

A keen diver, scuba diving satisfies my yearning for adventure and immersing into the unknown. The ocean can, at once, contain dangerous shipwrecks and beautiful reefs, treacherous sharks and playful dolphins.

For me, scuba diving offers a beautiful metaphor for diving into the deep ocean of the inner Self that can nourish the soul but also hold paradoxes, just like the many facets of our own beautiful being.

My years and years of soul searching have resulted in this, my first trilogy, *Karma & Diamonds*.

# Karma & Diamonds

## Book 2 - Web of Karma

### "Will dramatic revelations about lives long past finally free her to be happy?"

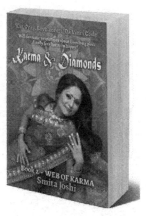

Smita embarks impulsively on her India trip, purely guided by her intuition. Starting with a visit to distant Indian family, she soon finds herself on a trip to the foothills of the Himalayas with doctors, one of whom is also a well-respected spiritual *guru*. By day, they serve the under-privileged by giving them free eye operations and at night, stay in *ashrams*, where the *guru* gives daily teachings.

It is then that she discovers that what she calls her 'Inner Diamond', is curiously connected to the core teachings of ancient India, as if she had already received this age-old knowledge through other means. She walks the fire and participates in sacred ceremonies.

Back in London, she hopes she is now ready to accelerate her business career and enter into a serious romantic relationship. But then, her Diamond starts revealing to her all kinds of mysterious clues once again. She has a sudden, inexplicable urge to create peculiar paintings, which she will later discover are in fact sacred *mandalas*. She is guided to a special book in the British Library, the significance of which she will only discover later on.

She realises that these are pieces of her past lives that are starting to emerge and that compel her to explore her long lost past. The Diamond takes her to New Mexico, where she meets a remarkable woman who guides her to relive several tragic past lives. She will discover a horrible truth that has had her and her mother spellbound for centuries and she is catapulted into a special moment in history where romance, science and mysticism meet.

Now better understanding her *karma*, she realises her trip to India was not complete and she needs to go back once more, this time, for a special encounter.

Back home in London, when she thinks she's finally free of her age-old *karma*, ready to live a happy and fulfilled life, she gets devastating news that, for years, a fatal disease has been quietly festering in her abdomen. Doctors refuse to operate, as they believe it's too late.

Will all her struggle and quests have been for nothing?

# Karma & Diamonds

## Book 3 - Diamond Revealed

### "Will a life-threatening condition bring her quest to a premature end?"

Refusing to die, Smita calls once more onto her Inner Diamond to guide her. It takes her to the one doctor in the world who dares to operate on her.

No sooner is she back from hospital that she sees an angel-bird in her meditation. It tells her the quest is not complete. More work is to be done and she is to go to Hawaii if she is to find freedom and fulfilment.

In Hawaii, reality and higher realms seem to merge as she witnesses many mystical events. On the volcano she meets the angel-bird again and he clears her path to encounter the goddess whom she has already encountered in her dreams.

She is taken to swim with wild dolphins in the ocean off the coast of Hawaii. They accept her into their pod and through their joyful leaf ritual, they grant her permission to be playful again.

She experiences a mysterious phenomenon at the stunning Shiva temple in Kauai, which the priests explain as a rare and precious blessing.

Loose ends still remain. When she returns back home, her intuition compels her to visit, in the nick of time, the one key person in her life with whom a significant completion must take place if she is to be at peace with her past.

This time, the cycles of *karma* seem finally complete and she can have an emotional reconciliation with her mother and those closest to her.

She is now liberated to soar at work and soon afterwards she meets a man who intrigues her. She certainly is ready for a beautiful partnership now. But will he capture her heart? Will she be able to find true love?